D0852847

# Raising
# Your
# Type A
# Child

# Raising Your Type A Child

*How to Help Your Child Make the Most of an Achievement-Oriented Personality*

**DR. STEVEN SHELOV
and JOHN KELLY**

POCKET BOOKS

New York   London   Toronto   Sydney   Tokyo   Singapore

The ideas, procedures and suggestions in this book are intended to supplement, not replace, the medical advice of a trained health professional. All matters regarding your child's health require medical supervision. Consult your child's physician before adopting the suggestions in this book, as well as about any condition that may require diagnosis or medical attention. The author and publishers disclaim any liability arising directly or indirectly from the use of this book.

 POCKET BOOKS, a division of Simon & Schuster Inc.
1230 Avenue of the Americas, New York, NY 10020

Copyright © 1991 by Dr. Steven P. Shelov and John Kelly

All rights reserved, including the right to reproduce
this book or portions thereof in any form whatsoever.
For information address Pocket Books, 1230
Avenue of the Americas, New York, NY 10020

Shelov, Steven P.
   Raising your type A child : how to help your child make the most of an achievement-oriented personality / Steven Shelov and John Kelly.
      p.   cm.
   Includes bibliographical references and index.
   ISBN 0-671-69245-3
   1. Parent and chld—United States.   2. Child-rearing—United States.   3. Type A behavior in children—United States.   I. Kelly, John, 1945–   .  II. Title.
HQ755.85.S52   1991
649′.1—dc20                                          91-18640
                                                         CIP

First Pocket Books hardcover printing September 1991

10   9   8   7   6   5   4   3   2   1

POCKET and colophon are registered trademarks of
Simon & Schuster Inc.

Printed in the U.S.A.

*This book is dedicated to those researchers who have helped clarify the qualities and characteristics of Type A children and their families, and to the promise inherent in all such children.*

# CONTENTS

Introduction                                                    *1*

**1** The Child Everyone Notices                               *3*

## PART ONE
## The Making of a Type A Child

**2** Origins of Negative Type A Behavior                      *15*

**3** The Superachiever, The Critic, and The Hurrier:
The Type A and His Family                                      *29*

**4** Iron Man and King of the Hill: The Type A and
Significant Others                                            *55*

**5** "Whoever Has the Most Toys When He Dies,
Wins:" The Type A in Society                                  *74*

**6** The Angry Heart                                          *91*

## PART TWO
## The Making of a
## Type A Positive Child

Introduction                                                  *105*

**7** A Few Words About Some Old Habits and How to
Eliminate Them                                               *107*

**8** Setting Goals for a Type A    *118*

**9** How to Talk to a Type A Child    *134*

**10** Teaching a Type A Child Right from Wrong: Respect-Oriented Discipline    *154*

**11** Changing Type A's Values    *168*

**12** Teaching a Type A How to Manage His High-Strung Temperament    *184*

Bibliography    *201*

Index    *209*

# INTRODUCTION

Early in his life, you probably sensed that your child was a little different. He or she may have seemed a little more energetic, ambitious, intelligent, and perhaps high-strung than other youngsters. You probably also sensed that raising him or her would pose special challenges. You're not alone. These feelings are common among the parents of the Type A boys and girls I work with.

What brings these mothers and fathers to me for help is my experience in working with Type A children. As Professor of Pediatrics and Associate Vice Chairman of the Pediatrics Department at Albert Einstein Medical College in New York City, I've spent a great deal of my professional time working with Type A boys and girls. In the early 1980s, this work, which, like most clinical work, had been largely informal and ad hoc, began to take on a more rigorous and formal structure. Concerned by a spate of social changes that seemed to me to put the Type A child at special risk, I decided to begin incorporating my clinical experiences and observations into a series of strategies and techniques that I felt could be used by the parents of all Type A's.

If these strategies can be said to have a single aim, it is to allow the remarkable Type A child (and Type A's are among America's best and brightest youngsters) to enjoy all the very real benefits of his fast-track personality while avoiding its equally real hazards. And if these techniques arise largely from my own clinical experiences, their shape and form have been influenced by the contributions of a number of colleagues and associates. These include Dr. Maria Alba Fisch and Dr. Marsha Liberman Shelov, both of whom have been an invaluable re-

1

source both in my work with Type A patients and in the preparation of this book; researchers Karen Matthews of the University of Pittsburgh, Carl Thorenson of Stanford University, and Redford Williams of Duke University, whose pioneering work has had a profound influence on my thinking about the Type A child and the unique developmental risks he faces.

I'd also like to thank my colleagues at Albert Einstein Medical College; in particular, those in the Department of Behavioral Pediatrics, whose counsel and understanding have been a constant source of support in the work that led to this book.

And, finally, I'd like to thank my patients and their parents for allowing me to use their experiences. However, to protect their privacy, I've changed their names, backgrounds and physical characteristics.

—Dr. Steven Shelov

# The Child Everyone Notices

## Who is the Type A child?

He is Billy, who, though only 4, exudes such an air of leadership that when the group of preschoolers he's been placed with are asked to pick a leader for their games, all eyes immediately turn to newcomer Billy.

## Who is the Type A child?

She is 6-year-old Pam and already she looks so competent that when adult observers who've been watching her and other youngsters perform competitive-oriented tasks are asked, "Which child in the group do you think is the most intelligent and able?," Pam is everyone's first choice.

## Who is the Type A child?

He is Tommy, who, at age 7 is so motivated and focused that when exposed to noisy disruptions, he is the only child in his study group with enough concentration to finish his assigned task.

## Who is the Type A child?

He and she are everything you'd imagine a Type A to be—bright, ambitious, energetic, aggressive, and of course competitive. He and she are tomorrow's doctors, lawyers, business executives, labor leaders, artists, entrepreneurs, politicians, and engineers—in other words, he and she are among America's most promising children. And therein lies the reason why new research on the Type A child has such importance, not only for the Type A's parents, teachers, and other significant adult figures in his life, but for all of us who care about the future of American society.

Fittingly enough, this new research had its starting point in the acclaimed best-seller *The Type A Behavior Pattern & Your Heart*, and the questions it raised about the origins and the familial and social forces that shape Type A's.

### HOW THE TYPE A DIFFERS FROM OTHER CHILDREN

Over the past fifteen years, studies on youngsters like Pam and Billy have taught us a great deal about America's millions of Type A boys and girls.

We know, for example, that they are innately more energetic, focused, high-strung, and perhaps more intelligent than their peers. We also know that, as with Pam and Billy, they are likely to be perceived as much more leaderly, in charge, and competent than other youngsters.

We've learned as well that Type A's often face a different set of risks. The most notable and publicized of these, of course, is the long-term risk of heart disease. But the new research shows that well before cardiac malfunction becomes a danger, the Type A's high-strung temperament *and* the unusual reactions he elicits in others already have put him at risk for a host of unique social, psychological, emotional, and in some cases even academic problems.

Finally, we've learned that the Type A's development generally follows one of two courses. The first—and more familiar—of these has its unhappy endpoint in an angry, hypercompetitive, coronary-prone middle age. One of the major surprises to emerge from the research is just how early this course is set. Recent studies show that it isn't at all unusual for a 4-, 5-, or 6-

year-old to begin displaying the excessive achievement striving and hypercompetitiveness usually associated with 30- and 40-year-old Type A's; studies also show that it isn't unusual for 12- and 13-year-olds to display the elevated blood pressure and cholesterol levels associated with the behavior pattern.

The other possible ending for the Type A's story is a big—and happy—surprise. Recent studies, such as one on a group of award-winning Type A scientists, show that some Type A's learn how to make their fast-track personalities work for, rather than against, them. Not surprisingly, the research shows that the ability to do this is developed in childhood and is fostered by a mother and father who understand the special challenges of parenting a Type A child.

Simply put, the goal of this book is to show you how to provide that kind of parenting by revealing what we've learned recently about the remarkable Type A and the kind of environment he needs to be all that he can be.

## IS YOUR CHILD A TYPE A?

If you find yourself checking off six or more of the following questions, which are part of a larger scale developed by Dr. Karen Matthews of the University of Pittsburgh, then your youngster possesses the temperamental marker called "physiological reactivity," which underlies the Type A behavior pattern.

1. When my child plays, he or she is competitive. _____
2. My child appears to be a natural leader. _____
3. When working or playing, my child always tries to outdo other children. _____
4. My child becomes impatient while waiting for others. _____
5. My child does things in a hurry. _____
6. My child is quick-tempered. _____
7. My child becomes irritated easily. _____
8. My child performs better when competing with others. _____
9. My child works quickly and energetically, rather than slowly and deliberately. _____

10. My child likes to argue and debate. _____
11. My child has trouble sitting still for prolonged periods of time. _____

As Dr. Matthews' scale suggests, physiological reactivity accounts for a lot of behaviors we think of as typically Type A. It is, for example, the source of much of the A's eye-catching drive and energy and, perhaps, competitive exuberance and achievement orientation, as well as his being high-strung, which makes him unusually prone to anger, anxiety, and impatience. But, as we shall see later in this book, it is the physiologically reactive child's environment which plays a major role in determining the eventual shape these biologically based traits take and the role they come to play in his personality.

Like the award-winning Type A scientists in the study I mentioned on page 5, when a reactive youngster receives the special support and understanding he needs, all that is best in his personality emerges. But when he doesn't, more often than not the result is the classic Type A behavior pattern and the five characteristics that define it: anger, hostility, impatience, hypercompetitiveness, and a predisposition to coronary heart disease.

THE DEVELOPMENT OF NEGATIVE TYPE A BEHAVIOR

How these traits develop is perhaps the key finding to emerge from the new research (I'll examine their roots in detail in chapter 2). And the process that fosters these traits works something like this: Research shows that the competent, energetic, leaderly behavior of Type A's like Billy and Pam make them not only standouts in any group but the target of unusually high expectations and demands. Parents, teachers, caregivers, peers, and even perfect strangers have been found to expect—and indeed demand—things of the competent, assured-looking Type A boy or girl that they don't demand of less able-looking children. In the classroom, for example, the Type A child will immediately be pegged as an A (and not a B) student, and on the playing field as a superior athlete. In the home, he's often saddled with responsibilities other children his age are able to avoid.

This unusual environmental response is an important factor in promoting negative Type A behavior because the anger, the hypercompetitiveness, the proneness to heart disease—all the traits that make the behavior pattern so worrisome—originate in the innately competitive, high-strung, and—as we shall see later—often insecure A's desire to live up to the high hopes he inspires in those around him.

As long ago as the early 1970s, researchers speculated that the larger environment—the society we live in and the values we live by—might also foster negative Type A behavior. As we shall see in chapter 5, a growing body of evidence now supports this conclusion. Increasingly, the ways we define success to our children, the role models we hold up to them, and the stresses we place them under are being viewed as culprits that not only enhance vulnerability to negative Type A behavior but, these days, make such behavior common at an alarmingly early age.

Consider, for example, the reactions of the 3- and 4-year-old Type A's who took part in toy car races organized by Dr. Tiffany Field and her colleagues at the University of Miami. Unlike their peers who responded to losses the way preschoolers usually do—by briefly sulking and then forgetting about it—these A's had already developed such out-of-control achievement drives that their losses produced ferocious temper tantrums. After a defeat, each A would immediately leap up and rush over to the corner, where Dr. Field had wisely placed a plastic Bobo doll, and begin flailing at the doll.

### BUILDING A POSITIVE ENVIRONMENT FOR TYPE A's

Recent research has identified the environmental elements that allow a child like Pam or Billy to enjoy the benefits of his Type A personality while avoiding its very real emotional, psychological, and physical hazards. These elements fall into two categories. The first, which I call Esteem Builders, are important because they act as an antidote to the pernicious sense of insecurity that is the starting point for negative Type A behavior.

What are these Esteem Building elements?

*Open, honest communication* is the first. It promotes high self-esteem for a very simple reason: it makes the Type A feel that his thoughts, feelings, and opinions are respected and understood, even if they don't win parental approval and agreement.

*Positive, respect-oriented discipline* is the second element. This promotes self-worth for an equally simple reason: it shows the Type A that while Mom and Dad may not like what he did, they still love and respect him.

An ability to set *realistic, attainable goals* is the third element. If you spent time observing the Type A boys and girls I work with, I think you'd agree with me: Of all the Esteem Builders, this is one of the most important to the Type A, because it most directly touches on his sense of self.

The second category of environmental elements that have been associated with the promotion of positive Type A behavior might be described as Perspective Builders. Given his innate drives, the expectations he elicits in others, and the values his society promotes, many 5- or 6-year-old Type A's have already arrived at the conclusion that winning is the only thing that matters.

Perspective Builders act as an antidote to such single-mindedness because they promote a more balanced and healthy view of life. My work suggests that three in particular are most important.

*The presence of positive parental role models* is the first. It derives from the observation that in homes where parents behave in ways that say, "Success is important, but it's not the only important thing in life," children are able to develop other ways to fill their self-esteem needs.

*Participation in community and family activities* is the second element, and it's important for a reason that often surprises parents. Such activities provide a way of helping a competitive, achievement-minded child discover something that he or she often has trouble discovering alone: that doing things for others can soothe you when you're angry, lift your heart when you're low, and help you when you're confused.

The third important Perspective Builder is *parental awareness of our society's increasingly Type A-ogenic values.* American culture always has been notorious for its promotion of such values, especially in the last decade. Everywhere a child looks today, he observes greed, selfishness, and narcissism being celebrated. As Stanford psychologist Carl Thorenson noted recently, these characteristics can bring out the worst in a Type A boy or girl, unless someone points out the danger of such traits.

Not coincidentally, an ongoing study by Dr. Karen Matthews has found many of these environmental elements present in the homes of her Type A's who have learned how to make their competitive, achievement-oriented personalities work for, rather than against, them.

A major goal of this book is to show you how to create these six elements in your home. To give you an idea of the difference they can make in your Type A's development, consider the difference they made in 9-year-old Ben Leventhal's.

On his first visit to my office, Ben, who like many Type A's is a bright, energetic child, displayed all the signs of a youngster who has developed the negative aspects of the behavior pattern. There were constant complaints from Ben's teachers about his monopoly of classroom discussions and fidgety impatience, from his friends and peers about his chip-on-the-shoulder hostility, and from just about everyone about his brash, aggressive hypercompetitiveness. What worried Marge and Sam Leventhal most was Ben's anger and the disruptive acting out it produced.

Just about anything could send Ben into an epic temper tantrum. Once the furies were upon him, woe be to bystanders, however innocent. Once, in such a state, Ben had thrown his best friend's Nintendo set on the floor. Another time, he threw a cantaloupe across the dining room table at his sister, Sarah.

However, as Marge and Sam learned how to create a family environment where the six positive Type A elements were present, Ben's negative behavior patterns were gradually replaced by the traits that mark a child who has learned to make the most of his fast-track personality. Ben learned how to:

- Lose without losing his temper
- Compete without bruising the ego or feelings of others
- Lead without arousing animosity and jealousy
- Say "no" to unrealistic goals and challenges
- Share
- Wait without becoming impatient
- Derive a sense of validation from loving and being loved by others, rather than just from outperforming them

In the year I worked with Ben, another important change was that his high-for-his-age blood pressure normalized. As we shall see in chapter 6, this turnaround illustrates one of the recent discoveries about the link between heart disease and the Type A personality: The elements that promote healthy emotional and psychological growth in a Type A child also promote a healthy heart.

Some notable changes also occurred among the elder Leventhals. Sam and Marge became less critical of Ben, less likely to tell him how to do things, and stopped comparing his achievements to those of his friends. Most important, they learned to set realistic expectations and goals for their Type A son. In other words, they stopped using many of the parental behaviors that have been associated with promoting negative Type A behavior in a child.

Much of the parental guilt that was so evident in my first meetings with the Leventhals began to dissipate. This change was particularly evident in Marge, who, like many parents of Type A's, had spent a good deal of time wondering why her palpably bright, talented child was so problem-prone, and who had concluded that the fault lay in her own inadequate parenting.

What Marge learned over the course of her visits with me—and what you will learn in this book—is that this conclusion is wrong. When a Type A child develops problems, their roots lie not in inadequate or insensitive parenting but in the knowledge gaps that prevent a parent from providing his child with the special nurturing he requires to be all that a Type A can be.

Although we have learned a great deal about these needs over the past decade and a half, virtually none of this important information has filtered down to those who need it most— parents like you.

As the first book to close the knowledge gap between laboratory and home, *Raising Your Type A Child* draws on material from two sources. The first is the research on these remarkable youngsters; in terms of the boys and girls it affects and can benefit, this work represents one of the most important and exciting bodies of pediatric knowledge to emerge in the past quarter-century. The other source of knowledge is my personal experience. In my capacity as Professor of Pediatrics at Albert

Einstein College of Medicine and in my clinical capacity as a physician, I've worked with a great many Type A children and their parents. Out of my work has come a series of techniques and strategies that can help transform a child into what I call a "Type A positive." To understand why this is such an important need, let's look at the developmental course most Type A children currently follow.

# PART
# I

♦

# The Making
# of a
# Type A Child

# 2

# Origins of Negative Type A Behavior

## Who is the classic Type A child?

- He often resists praise.
- He's a scorekeeper who closely monitors the achievements of friends and peers.
- He has difficulty reaching out and asking for help.
- He frequently does more than he's asked or needs to do.
- In games, he insists on taking his turn first.
- Even when he's busy, he'll take on new commitments.
- He frequently does two, three, or four things at once.
- He gets into arguments and fights with other children.
- He sets unrealistically high standards for himself.
- In certain circumstances, he displays blood pressure and cholesterol levels that are high for his age.
- He has an insatiable desire to win.
- Even when he does win, he feels as if he lost.

There's one other thing you should know about the classic Type A, because it explains a lot not only about these behaviors but about his personality in general. Beneath his often cocky, brash, self-assured exterior, the classic A is a deeply insecure child.

I know that *insecurity* is a charged word for parents; they immediately associate it with their own failings. But the Type A's self-doubts arise from another source. They are linked not to the failures of insensitive, uncaring parents, but to the qualities that make the Type A boy and girl different from other children.

### ORIGINS OF INSECURITY: ATTACHMENT DISRUPTIONS

One of the origins of insecurity is biological. Being reactive or high-strung, the Type A feels physical and emotional discomfort more sharply than do other youngsters. Once aroused, these feelings are much harder to soothe and comfort. What links this physiological peculiarity to the A's insecurity is the vulnerability it creates to attachment disruptions. Attachment, which bonds parent and child together in the first critical years of life, is universally recognized as *the* key building block of a strong, secure, robust "I." This is because the thousands of small acts of parental sensitivity that make up the attachment process create a healthy sense of self-importance.

As the child discovers that his parents know how to soothe him when he's upset, feed him when he's hungry, and calm him when he's overexcited, he begins to interpret these parental behaviors as: "I must be a very important person to deserve such considerate treatment." As this happy thought grows, so too grows the tremendous sense of security it confers.

However, because very little that Mom and Dad do can make a highly reactive infant feel comforted, it's very likely that he will come to a different conclusion about his worthiness.

Exactly why such infants have a low comfort index is unclear, but recent research by Dr. Jaak Panksepp of Bowling Green University suggests that it may be linked to an otherwise benign genetic peculiarity. Dr. Panksepp's studies indicate that reactive infants (and children) may secrete so little of the body's natural tranquilizer, brain opinoids, that they're physically incapable of experiencing the sense of relief and soothing that fosters a strong, secure attachment and a strong, secure sense of self.

## THE TYPE A EFFECT AND INSECURITY

The other major source of the Type A child's insecurity is the Type A effect. This originates in what's called the A's aura of competence or take-chargeness. It wasn't just coincidental that Type A Pam, the child I mentioned at the beginning of chapter 1, was picked as the best puzzle-solver by the adult observers in her study group. Research shows that even peers perceive the Type A to be smarter, more competent, decisive, motivated, leaderly, and responsible than other children. In a recent University of California study, children at a summer camp were asked to pick the best leaders and athletes in their respective groups. When investigators checked, they found that most of the youngsters chosen were Type A's.

Many researchers believe that the competent, I'm-in-charge manner that guided these campers' choices is a reflection of the Type A's reactivity, which makes him both high-strung and eye-catchingly energetic. But another contributing factor may be superior intelligence. Not everyone agrees on this point, but a study by the University of Pittsburgh's Dr. Karen Matthews does show that Type A's regularly outscore Type B's on school tests.

My own thinking on this point, which is shared by Dr. Carl Thorenson, Professor Emeritus of Psychology at Stanford University, is that the Type A's aura of competence also reflects his insecure attachment. We knew that a large part of what makes Type A's so eye-catching is their desire to win. And not uncommonly, insecure boys and girls adopt such a strategy to disguise their self-doubts and insecurities.

The "Type A effect" refers to the unusually high expectations and demands that the A's aura of competence elicits from others. A good example of how it contributes to his insecurity was provided by a strange-situation test I witnessed recently. The purpose of such tests is to gauge the reaction of a child's personality on a strange adult. Patty Kauffman, the able-looking 10-year-old Type A in the experiment, had an immediate and dramatic effect on Ilse O'Connor, the graduate student who acted as her adviser during a math test. While the graduate students partnered with the Type B children confined their assistance to low-key advice. Under the sway of the Type A effect, however, Ilse reacted the way other adults have in similar studies: she transformed herself into a combination cheerleader and taskmaster.

### PARENTS AND THE TYPE A EFFECT

Not surprisingly, those in the child's immediate circle are even more susceptible to the Type A effect. This susceptibility tends to be especially pronounced in the Type A's parents, whom studies describe as:

• Middle class, urban, or suburban
• Often (although not always) possessed of a high achievement need of their own
• Especially prone to the American success ethic
• Vulnerable to parental guilt

Studies also show that under the sway of the Type A effect, such parents:

• Develop a unique set of expectations about the child and who he should be, which I call "sky-high goals"
• Often, overencourage, overcriticize, and overpraise
• Rate their child's performance in terms of what are called *social comparisons* (That is, they judge the A's performance not on his ability to attain a goal, but on whether he attained it faster—or in some other way better—than other children.)

The image these points conjure up is that of a parent like the father in the recent movie *Parenthood*, who was so relentlessly achievement-minded that he was constantly "at" his 3-year-old daughter with flash cards, multiplication tables, and any other educational device he could find. But the picture of the Type A's parent that emerges from the assembled research, and from my experience, is more nuanced and much gentler.

The overencouragement, overcriticism, and social comparisons look very blatant when taken out of context and reduced to a series of bite-sized bullets, yet these are only a part—and usually a small part—of the loving behaviors that flow from parent to Type A child in the course of a day. And just as often, these behaviors are activated by subtle psychological forces that unconsciously play on the parent's sense of guilt and responsibility.

One of the most important of these forces is the culture in which we live and the often far-too-high premium it puts on Type A values such as winning, success, and being number one. Day in and day out, year in and year out, society tells parents that these are the only meaningful goals in life. Thus, it's only natural that when a child possesses the attributes the culture deems those of a "born winner," the parent feels a special responsibility to help the child be all he can—even if it means pushing him a little.

Another subtle influence on the behavior of the Type A's parents is the often formidable nature of their child's ambitions. You can catch a glimpse of this characteristic in a study where 8-year-old A's and B's were asked to hold a five-pound weight. The moment they tired, the B's, in sensible Type B fashion, put down their weights. But not the A's; they held on and on to their weights. Outside the laboratory, the research shows that, in effect, the drive these 8-year-old A's displayed conditions a parent to be demanding. The child asks so much of himself that the parent begins to think (usually without realizing it) that perhaps she should encourage him to get a 95 instead of an 85 on next week's math test. Or, that she should enroll him in a computer class after school, even though he already has karate, pottery, and gymnastics after school. Or that perhaps he can take care of himself after school, even though he is only 9 or 10.

### SIGNIFICANT OTHERS AND THE TYPE A EFFECT

Because they, too, live in the American success culture, and because of the Type A child's special characteristics, his caregivers, teachers, and peers also are susceptible to the Type A effect. In fact, my first encounter with its ability to elicit great expectations came not from a mother or father but from a caregiver. As she ushered her young charge into my office one bitterly cold morning, she began chiding him for forgetting his mittens. Once we were alone, I gently pointed out to the caregiver that this was asking a lot of a 4-year-old.

"Oh, no, you don't understand, Dr. Shelov," she replied. "Timmy's smarter than other children his age. If he's forgotten his mittens, it's because he's being lazy."

When this incident occurred twelve years ago, I thought her behavior odd enough to mention it to the child's parents. But a recent Kansas State University study indicates that caregivers generally are susceptible to the Type A effect. That is, a caregiver also will form the expectation that the able child in her care should not just do well, but very well, and he or she will also express that expectation in behavior such as overencouragement.

The caregivers in the KSU study responded in this way when a Type A child accomplished a study goal. Instead of congratulating him, the way the Type B's caregivers did their charges, they would immediately praise the A past the goal by telling him, in effect, "All right, that was good, but I think you can do even better. Why don't you see if you can do the task faster next time."

Dr. Carol Whelan of the University of California has found that teachers also appear vulnerable to the Type A effect; they regularly judge their Type A students more competent than the Type B's and expect a correspondingly higher performance.

The evidence suggests that susceptibility to the effect extends to the Type A's peers and friends as well. For example, some of Dr. Whelan's research, as well as several other studies mentioned earlier indicate that other boys and girls are as likely to be impressed by the A's aura of competence and ability to take charge as adults are. In my experience, often this impression translates into a general peer expectation that the Type A is a good student, a popular social figure, or—in the case of Samantha Barnes, one of my 9-year-old A's—a superior athlete.

Sam's encounter with this expectation about her athletic prowess occurred during her first day at camp last summer. She was standing by the pool with three other girls, when one of them suddenly pointed to the high diving board and said to Sam, who radiates the Type A's aura of competence, "I'll bet you've been off the high board lots of times." In fact, Sam had never dived off a high board in her life, but she didn't let that stop her from taking up the implicit challenge in her new friend's remark.

The lifeguard told her mother, Melissa, about the incident. He said that Sam had climbed up on the board with great dash and, for a novice, made a very respectable dive. But everyone, including Type A's, and especially 9-year-old A's, has a breaking point. The dive brought Sam to hers. As soon as she climbed out of the pool, she ran to the lifeguard and burst into tears.

## SKY-HIGH GOALS AND THE DEVELOPMENT OF NEGATIVE TYPE A BEHAVIOR

When Melissa Barnes told me this story, I could tell she was puzzled as well as upset by her daughter's behavior. But there is a simple explanation for it, and it brings us to the chief danger of the Type A effect: the sky-high goal-setting style it produces in those around the A.

While every environment sets goals for a child, the goals the Type A's environment (by environment, I mean principally parents, but also, to a lesser but still significant degree, caregivers and teachers) sets for him are unusual in two ways. The first is that they often are very high. If another child gets a 95, the able-looking Type A will be expected to get a 98. If another child takes computer and karate after school, the able-looking A will be expected to take computer, karate, *and* pottery after school. If another child is expected to endure a divorce with only a moderate amount of upset, the able-looking A will be expected to endure it with a minimum amount of upset.

The other unusual aspect of sky-high goals is that they are open-ended; success is defined in a vague, elusive way that always puts its attainment just beyond the child's reach. Sometimes this elusiveness is established very starkly by continually redefining what constitutes an achievement. If the child becomes top in his class, for example, suddenly success will be redefined as being top in the entire school. The caregivers in the Kansas State University study exemplified this phenomenon when, instead of congratulating their Type A charges on completing an assigned goal within a given period of time, they immediately redefined success as doing the task faster the next time.

Often open-endedness is established in a more subtle way. In this variation of a sky-high goal, success isn't continually redefined, it's just made to seem to be whatever the child hasn't achieved. Usually this is accomplished by the use of praise as well as criticism, which creates the impression that Mom or

Dad had something a little better in mind. For example, if the A draws a good picture or gets a good grade, he'll be praised, but in a way that leaves him feeling that more was hoped for—as in, "Gee, I love your picture, but you're *such* a talented artist, I'll bet you can do even better." (It's important to emphasize that such phrases become a factor in promoting negative behavior only when *consistently* used.) Or, like the Type A boys in a recent State University of New York study, he may simply be criticized for not doing better. Although these youngsters all successfully completed their assigned research tasks, and although they outperformed their Type B study-mates by a considerable margin, their fathers (who, not coincidentally, were all Type A men) chided them for not performing even more impressively.

Excessive achievement striving is the first Type A trait to emerge from the psychological dynamic established by sky-high goals. Because his insecurities and self-doubts create a strong craving for love and approval, the A pushes himself very hard in order to achieve his parents', teachers', and caregivers' goals. However, because those goals define success in such a high and open-ended way, his pursuit usually ends in failure, and this sets up a self-reinforcing cycle. Each failure leaves the child a little more insecure and self-doubting. Because these feelings are painful, the A pursues the next sky-high goal even more furiously, and, should that pursuit also fail, his insecurities deepen, which moves his achievement striving up one more notch.

As the Type A gets older, other sources begin to feed his achievement striving. Among them are his own goals. The targets children set for themselves are shaped by the ones their environment sets for them. If the environment says true success lies in the accomplishment you haven't yet achieved (no matter how impressive the ones you have achieved), eventually that standard will influence the goals the child sets for himself. What put Sam Barnes on that high diving board was not Melissa and Harry Barnes's sky-high goals, but her own.

In time, the larger society also begins to feed the A's striving. American society has its own version of sky-high goals, and, as we shall see in chapter 5, they possess an almost irresistible glamour for a child with the Type A's ambitions and insecurities.

The other traits that make up negative Type A behavior arise from the stresses produced by years of running in place after a vague, ill-defined idea of success. An important component in this aspect of the Type A's formation is the child's reactive or high-strung temperament. The greater the stress, the closer the A's always-volatile emotions come to the surface. Exactly at what stage achievement-related stresses reach the point of critical mass, where they begin producing negative Type A behaviors, varies from child to child. Children of ages 4, 3, and even 2 display occasional to frequent flashes of Type A anger, impatience, and hypercompetitiveness. However, the consensus among authorities is that it isn't until age 6 or so that a child begins to display consistently the negative traits that define the classic Type A personality.

These traits are:

*Anger and Hostility.* Pain causes anger in all human beings, and because feeling inadequate and insecure is painful—especially for a child—the major source of the A's anger is low self-esteem. This low self-esteem has its roots in the child's attachment experiences, but as he grows older, his sense of inadequacy begins to be fed by the goals set by his environment. The large reservoir of free-floating anger in 6-, 7-, and 8-year-old Type A's is a direct result of the child's insecurities resulting from these additional goals.

Even the most insignificant of defeats can ignite this volatile and raw anger. Think of what the Type A's in Dr. Tiffany Field's study did to the Bobo doll after losing a toy-car race. Or consider some of the things the summer campers in the University of California study had to say about their Type A camp mates. While these youngsters admired the A's leaderliness and athletic ability, they complained—in some cases heatedly—about the A's habit of erupting at even the smallest setback.

The picture of the Type A child's anger that emerges from these and other recent studies is of volcaniclike eruptions. In the face of defeat, the Type A either loses his temper or, like the girls in a study at the University of Stockholm, becomes loud, boisterous, or aggressive. Dr. Lars Bergman, the researcher who conducted this study, believes that his findings indicate that in Type A's, as in other children, anger is sex-mediated. Vesuviuslike eruptions are acceptable in males but not in females. So, rather than blow up, Type A girls act out their anger in loud, disruptive, aggressive behavior.

At times, instead of exploding outwardly, a defeated A will direct his anger inward, at himself. Mike Traub, a boy who played short stop on my Little League team last summer, is a case in point. Mike is a talented baseball player, but he is not the great baseball player of his father's mind's eye. Mike is aware of this "perfect" version of himself, and he expresses his anger at not being him in a form of self-punishment. Mike refuses to accept compliments, even for the things he does well.

Several times last summer, when I tried to compliment him on a good catch or critical hit, Mike either turned my praise aside or turned it against himself by reminding me of his last error or last strikeout.

Children (and adults) who don't like themselves also don't like other children (and adults). Thus, to a significant degree, the Type A's hostility (which is usually defined as a wariness and distrust of others) is an expression of his feelings about himself. In time, the A's free-floating anger colors his perceptions of everything, including his friends and peers, whom he begins to view as a potential source of harm. One common expression of this Type A hostility and distrust is the A's reluctance to ask others for help. Another is the A's tendency to impute negative motives to even the most innocent behavior of friends.

A third expression of anger is exemplified by Mike Traub's reaction to a joke a teammate made about his new spike haircut. Instead of laughing off the remark, which was a harmless tease, Mike was so enraged that he went after the boy with a bat.

Dr. Redford Williams, Professor of Medicine at Duke University, believes that Type A hostility like Mike's might have a biological component—the same one that makes the Type A vulnerable to attachment disruptions: low opinoid secretion. Dr. Williams hypothesizes that this deficit may, over time, make people such a source of discomfort and unease to the Type A that an association forms in his mind: "People make me feel bad; therefore, I'd better be a little wary and suspicious of them."

*Hypercompetitiveness.* There aren't many direct cause-and-effect relationships in human development. However, one that does exist is that wins and victories are such an important antidote to self-doubts that an insecure boy or girl will do nearly anything to attain them. This explains quite a bit about the Type A's hypercompetitiveness.

For instance, it explains why the Type A never plays just to play—in other words, just for the fun of it. Whether it's a toy-car race or a baseball game, the A's play always has an element of deadly earnestness about it, and, given the stakes he imagines himself playing for, it isn't hard to understand why.

It also explains why such youngsters tend to turn everything, including even discussing baseball cards or walking to school, into a contest.

Finally, it explains why the triumphs of friends and peers are monitored so closely. When this trait first came to light in the early 1970s, it puzzled researchers. Why, after every study, did the 5- and 6-year-old A's in the study groups come up and ask, "Who got the most problems right?" or, "Who did the test questions fastest?" After thinking about it for a while, however, investigators realized that the A's curiosity wasn't so mysterious after all. If a child sees every aspect of his life as a competitive event, he'll want to monitor the competition's progress as closely as he can.

For an explanation of why even very big and very new victories don't slacken the A's competitive appetite, however, you have to look beyond his insecurities to the sky-high goals set for him.

Goals define the parameters of success for a child. When they are finite and concrete, they allow the youngster who picks up his room or does his best on a test to tell himself: "I've just scored an esteem-building success, I can relax and enjoy myself." But when goals define success as whatever triumph one hasn't yet achieved, nothing the youngster does feels big or important or satisfying enough to allow him to say to himself: "Congratulations, you really are a special 8- [or 10- or 12-] year-old." So, he never feels he can stop competing, even for a moment.

A good example of how this phenomenon translates into day-to-day behavior is provided in a story I heard from Barbara

Jorgenson, the mother of one of my 16-year-old Type A's. The morning after her daughter Sandra scored an important win at a high school track meet, Barbara found Sandra's bed empty when she went to wake her for an eight o'clock ballet class. Where could her daughter be at 7:15 on a Saturday morning? At 9:00, the mystery resolved itself; a sweaty Sandra walked into the kitchen in her running gear and announced she'd been at the high school track since 6:30, practicing for next week's meet.

There's a postscript to Sandra's story, and it illustrates another important factor of the Type A's hypercompetitiveness. The burning desire to win games and other competitive events, and to score high on tests, often fosters such anxiety ("Will I win? What will happen if I don't?") that the A's ability to compete can be undermined. This phenomenon is called performance anxiety, and it undid Sandra in her next race. She was so tense that, coming around the first turn, she lost her balance, tripped, and fell, and finished thirteenth in a field of fourteen.

Sandra's behavior at the Jorgensons' dinner table that night provides a good example of something else—how negative Type A behavior traits interact with one another. When younger brother Philip made a (mild, I'm told) joke about his sister's next-to-last-place showing, Sandra got so angry that she picked up a fork and threw it at him, then burst into tears.

*Impatience.* In the mind of an insecure child, most activities are perceived as a form of achievement. Belonging to the school fencing club, the debating team, and the honor-roll society provide the youngster with a way of demonstrating to himself and others how worthy he is. If the child also has been raised in a home that defines goals the way most Type A homes do, then very likely he won't join just those clubs but every other club and organization he can find until he becomes like the Type A teens in a recent study. These youngsters were committed to 50 percent more extracurricular activities than their Type B friends.

This activity level is a factor in the A's impatience because when you've got the same amount of time as your friends but 50 percent more to do and a high-strung temperament, a great sense of time urgency develops. Some very common Type A behaviors derive from this urgency.

One is an impulse to save time by doing two, three, or four things at once. If you followed a busy Type A teen, you would see what I mean. As you observed him in fencing class, you would notice the A reading his notes for the computer class that follows fencing, and checking his gear for tonight's basketball game.

You would also be struck by the hurriedness of the Type A teen's walk and the rapidfire quality of his speech, and would probably be annoyed by his tendency to keep interrupting you, which are some of the characteristics of impatient Type A boys and girls.

In the course of your time together, you would also notice that in an effort to save time, your impatient companion often raced through familiar tasks and assignments. And you might conclude—as many researchers have—that a principal reason for the Type A's poor performance is that, in his rush to do all he has to do, he cuts corners, doing tasks and assignments in a slap-dash manner. (Research shows that many Type A's do not do well academically.)

*A predisposition to coronary heart disease.* To understand how this risk originates and why it casts a shadow over the Type A child's future, it's necessary to understand how his biology and personality interact to create it. We'll take a closer look at this connection in chapter 6, but essentially it works like this: While all of us experience increases in blood pressure and cholesterol levels in moments of stress, because the A's reactivity makes him more high-strung, his blood pressure and cholesterol levels rise much more sharply at such moments and sharpest of all when stress evokes an angry or hostile response.

The recent discovery of the dramatic effect these traits have on the Type A's cardiovascular system has produced a major revision in the theory of Type A heart disease. Initially, it was thought that all negative Type A traits produced stresses great enough to create cardiac risk—that is, that impatience, hyper-competitiveness, and excessive achievement striving were cardiac-toxic. But recent research shows that only anger and hostility are.

Many researchers, however, don't believe this news is quite as good as it sounds. The reason: Even if only two of the behavior pattern's five components are cardiac toxic, those two—anger and hostility—are the ones most likely to be exacerbated by the Type A's peculiar combination of insecurities and excessive achievement striving. Thus, these traits alone will be enough to create an early risk of heart disease.

While the discovery of the link between heart disease and the Type A personality represents one of the most dramatic examples of somatization in the annals of medical history, a growing body of evidence indicates that cardiovascular disorders aren't the only form of somatization to which Type A boys and girls are vulnerable. A recent study by Dr. Jean Eagelton and her colleagues at the University of California at Santa Cruz shows that high Type A youngsters have a much greater incidence of headaches, stomach upsets, muscular tension, sleep problems, and faintness than other children. And a second recent study, by Lorna Hecht and her colleagues at the University of California at Santa Barbara, suggests that these and similar symptoms originate in the higher rates of depression and anxiety afflicting Type A boys and girls.

Taken together, these two pieces of research tell a worrisome story. They say that, long before heart disease becomes a danger, the stress of living up to everyone's sky-high expectations has exacted such a toll on the Type A child that his physical health is being undermined.

One last point:

Not all Type A's display the behaviors we've examined in this chapter to the same degree. Some are more angry than impatient, others more impatient than hypercompetitive. In still others, the predominant Type A characteristic will be performance anxiety or a tendency toward somatization. And while a number of factors produce these variations, a key factor is the parenting style of the A's mother and father.

# 3

# The Superachiever, The Critic, and The Hurrier: The Type A and His Family

Phillip Blondi likes to say that his wife, Joanne, makes a dramatic first impression, and I can't disagree with that. At our first meeting, Joanne nearly ran me over. Our near-collision occurred on a warm September afternoon in 1988. I was walking down the hall of a local New York television station with Allison Kahn, the young woman who produces my medical spots for the station's evening news, when suddenly out of an adjacent corridor a whirlwind of red curls in a green dress emerged and began bearing down on us at such a frantic clip, I half-expected it to produce a sonic boom as it whizzed by.

"That's Joanne Blondi," Allison whispered, as we watched the whirlwind descend on a group of visiting Japanese broadcasters farther down the hall. "She's one of the station's top news producers."

Over the next few months, most of the things I learned about Joanne fit the impression left by that first encounter. Joanne turned out to be energetic, intense, preoccupied, bright, and very ambitious. Once I became the Blondi family's pediatrician, I also learned that Joanne was a good example of the "Super-achiever," one of the parenting styles commonly associated with the promotion of negative Type A behavior.

**29**

Clinically, as we'll see later, the Superachiever style is defined by four specific characteristics. However, you can get a pretty good idea of the impulses that shape parents like Joanne from "Kids in the Fast Lane," a recent article in the *New York Times Sunday Magazine*. Author Sara Davidson, who numbers herself among the fast-track parents I call Superachievers, says such parents "are competitive, and time efficient. . ." [We] . . . "run on schedules and so do our kids."

According to Ms. Davidson, another distinguishing characteristic of Superachiever parents is their belief in the importance of early exposure to self-improvement courses of all kinds. "We compress [our children's] time and pack it with every imaginable type of enriching experience like camping and skiing. My husband studied karate in college, I did Tai Chi in my thirties, but our son is an orange belt at five."

Stylistically, the two other parents you'll meet in this chapter couldn't be more different from Superachievers like Joanne and Ms. Davidson. Joseph Cronin, the father in part 2, exemplifies the Critic, an almost exclusively male parenting style whose chief characteristic is, well, criticism. Rebecca Little, the mother in Part 3, is an example of the Hurrier. If Superachievers and Critics lean on their children to succeed, the Hurrier leans on hers for emotional support.

What links these three different parenting styles is that they are all characterized by the sky-high goal setting, which fosters negative Type A behavior in reactive children. What makes these styles relevant to you and other readers is that between them, they represent the forms of stresses common in Type A homes today. Like Superachiever Joanne Blondi and Critic Joe Cronin, millions of parents today expect and demand a very high level of achievement from their able-looking Type A's. And, like Hurrier Rebecca Little, millions more expect and demand an almost adultlike emotional competence from their equally capable-seeming Type A's.

While Joanne, Joe, and Rebecca are unusually pure examples, almost all Type A's parents have a little of the Superachiever, the Critic, and the Hurrier in them. So, in reading their stories, you'll learn how some of your actions may unwittingly be promoting negative Type A behavior in your child, and what you can do to correct them.

**Joanne Blondi: Superachiever**

At the station, people constantly marvel at Joanne's organizational skill and her flair for dramatizing the news. In a more florid form, these traits have been passed on to her 7-year-old Alexi. Small and dark, with lively eyes, a ring of curls, and a carnival barker's voice, Alexi is a natural showman, a pint-sized P.T. Barnum. Out of his fervid imagination flows an endless stream of ideas for shows and entertainments, and out of his quick brain, an equally endless stream of media and show business trivia. Alexi is the only 7-year-old I know who can tell you how much Jack Nicholson was paid for *Batman,* and what year *I Love Lucy* first aired.

The most fascinating thing about Alexi is the way he's used his impresario skills to overcome what, in a less imaginative and less intelligent child, would be a serious social handicap. Alexi doesn't like and shies away from the kinds of competitive activities other boys love and use as ways of relating. Sports, roughhousing, even the normally irresistible Nintendo bore him to the point of stupefaction.

However, Alexi has learned to make the things he does enjoy such fun for other children that his skills have become a vehicle for leadership and peer domination. Everyone wants to be Alexi's friend, and even more, everyone wants to be in Alexi's shows. When he created the Alexi Blondi Talent Show, for example, two of the most popular boys in his second-grade class almost came to blows over who would be Alexi's assistant. And when he organized the Alexi Blondi Magic Show (it is some measure of Alexi's Type A style that his name is attached to all his creations), there was such a stampede to be part of it that the parents of three classmates called Joanne to complain about their children's exclusion.

Quiet, stolid Phillip Blondi has spent the years since Alexi's birth in an almost perpetual state of bafflement. Where did he get such an astonishing son? he wonders. But Joanne knows. "I used to do the same kinds of things Alexi does when I was his age," she told me shortly after I became the family pediatrician.

What does baffle—and greatly worry—Joanne is the Type A Alexi. In areas like art, where he does choose to compete, Alexi is so hypercompetitive that when his teacher organized an art contest, he appeared in class with thirty packs of bubble gum and handed them out to the classmates who promised to vote his picture the best.

The Type A Alexi also can be so hostile that when a child offends him in even the slightest way, he will find some public way to humiliate him. He is also so anxious beneath his brash, self-assured exterior that even when he tries to sit still, he can't. As Phillip Blondi notes, even in front of the TV set, "Alexi bounces around like a Mexican jumping bean." Alexi's habit of freezing up when he is called on in class and his sleeping difficulties on nights before tests are further expressions of his free-floating anxiety.

This form of Type A behavior with a high anxiety component is common among reactive children of Superachiever parents. More often than not, it has its starting point in the Superachiever parent's very high success need. This need, which is a product of the parent's usually educated, middle-class background and high personal ambitions, not only increases her vulnerability to the Type A effect, but also influences the nature of the sky-high goals she sets. If these goals can be summarized, it would be: "I want my child to be number one, not just in math or in karate or baseball, but number one in everything."

Even more than words, a parent's style tells a child what Mom's and Dad's aspirations for him are. The four characteristics that make up the Superachiever's style italicize and underline the high premium the Superachiever puts on her child's becoming number one.

The characteristics are:

*Directiveness.* Put a Superachiever next to her child while he's performing a task (particularly a competitive task) and her desire for him to succeed will be so overwhelming she'll behave like the mothers and fathers in a recent Stanford University study, who on average offered *seventeen instructions per minute* to their Type A's while watching them compete with other subjects on a skills task.

*Intensity.* The intensity of the parental subjects who took part in the Stanford study is characteristic of the style, as well. According to its author, Dr. Paul Bracke, the parental subjects wanted their Type A children to outperform peers so badly that they not only told them how to do a thing, but grimaced and paced nervously while watching them do it.

*Social comparisons.* During his study, Dr. Bracke found that many of the parents also behaved like Ilse O'Connor, the young woman in the experiment I described in chapter 2.

These parents would monitor the progress of the other children in the study, then use what they had discovered to goad and spur their children on to greater efforts. Outside the laboratory, this trait manifests itself in the Superachiever's tendency always to ask her youngster, "How did your friend Billy do on that test?" or, "Who won the spelling bee?" According to Dr. Bracke, children are quick to catch the implicit Type A message of such social comparisons, which is: "In this house, success isn't measured by doing your best or completing an assigned task, but by the open-ended goal of being better than everyone else."

*Parent-oriented communication.* This form of communication isn't unique to Superachievers—to one degree or another, all parental styles associated with negative Type A behavior use it. But more than in any other style, Superachiever communication tends to revolve around the parent's perceptions of the child's needs and her hopes and dreams for him, *instead* of around the child's perceptions of his needs and his hopes and dreams for himself.

Taken together, these traits may make Superachievers sound domineering, even controlling, but in fact, like all parental styles, theirs has important strengths. One is that it makes a mother or father a valuable helpmate and ally, especially in moments of crisis. A case in point was the way Joanne eased Alexi's recovery from a broken leg last year.

Arriving in my office the week prior to the cast's removal, Alexi was full of trepidation. Would he be able to run or even walk without rebreaking the injured leg? he wondered. Such fears are very real to a child and can delay recovery by making him reluctant to use the injured limb.

One reason Alexi avoided this common pitfall was Joanne's directiveness, which in the weeks following the cast's removal made her an efficient, thoughtful, and tireless teacher. However, the Superachiever trait Alexi benefited most from during this difficult time was his mother's intensity. Joanne's desire to help her son regain a smooth, even stride was so palpable that it quite literally picked up Alexi and carried him over his fear. Nothing seemed too scary, as long as Joanne was there by his side, coaxing, cajoling, willing him to walk normally again.

The dramatic changes in Pilar, Alexi's caregiver, illustrate another Superachiever strength: their directiveness and intensity also make them excellent shapers and molders. Four years ago, Joanne's friends were surprised when she hired Pilar. Only 22, newly arrived in the United States from Guatemala and lacking any experience with children, Pilar seemed a questionable choice for Alexi. But Joanne saw these drawbacks as potential advantages. It would, she kept insisting to Phillip, to her mother, and to her friends, give her a chance to train a young woman whose caregiving skills would be tailored to Alexi's needs. Her confidence that she could provide the training paid off handsomely. These days, when friends mention Pilar to Joanne, it's usually to tell her how lucky she is to have such a wonderful caregiver for her son.

There are times, though, when Joanne's Superachiever style makes her son more prone to negative Type A behavior. Typical of this was her performance at one of Alexi's karate classes.

The first Superachiever trait to emerge during the class was social comparison. Seeing Alexi's friend Danny O'Neill walk into the gym with his mother, Joanne turned to Alexi and said, "Danny has a good form, I wish you'd work on yours a little more. You could be so good at karate, Alexi." A few minutes later, seeing Alexi's other friend Benny Pitchik sitting by the Coke machine, Joanne offered a few more observations. "Benny got his orange belt two weeks ago," she said. "Funny, I thought you'd get yours first." After Alexi changed into his *gee* (the traditional karate student's uniform), Joanne switched to directiveness. As Alexi paced nervously in front of her, Joanne reminded him: "Keep your head up, your back straight, and your left leg relaxed."

Five minutes later, stepping out onto the mat with his instructor, Alexi felt a palpable sense of relief. But no sooner had he assumed the traditional karate fighter's stance than a high, nasal voice rose above the din of the gymnasium to remind him: *"Remember, Alexi, keep that left leg relaxed!"*

How did Joanne's Superachiever behavior at the karate class help instill a high anxiety component in Alexi's negative Type A behavior?

Alexi's general Type A behavior owes much to his mother's use of social comparisons at the class—and everywhere else. In moderation, using friend Benny or Danny to make a point is harmless and can in some circumstances be beneficial. But when social comparisons are used constantly to judge a child's performance, in time their implicit messages—I want you to beat Danny and Benny in karate or in math—flow together in his mind to form a general sky-high goal: Mom (or Dad) expects him to beat Danny and Billy and everyone else at everything, all the time.

This message promotes negative Type A behavior in two ways. First, it sets off furious achievement striving. Being tops in a single activity is hard enough, but being tops in everything all the time is such a big and preoccupying job (especially if you are an insecure 8- or 10- or 12-year-old), how can a child ever hope to stop competing? The other major contribution social comparison makes to negative Type A behavior is as a source of anger. The almost malicious delight Alexi took in excluding three children from his magic show is a product not of innate meanness or low brain opinoid production, but of all the anger produced by his failure to live up to the impossible standard of success in his home.

The high anxiety that shapes Alexi's negative Type A behavior owes much to another Superachiever trait Joanne displayed at the karate class: instructiveness. While the intended effect of the Superachiever's advice and instruction is to help her child achieve her goal of being number one, its unintended effect is to undermine his confidence in his ability to achieve the goal on his own. The overly helpful parent always leaves a child wondering, "Who was really responsible for that success, me and my skill or Mom and Dad and their advice and instruction?" In an insecure Type A, this question will raise a second one: "How will I meet Mom's and Dad's goal without their help?" And then a third: "Will they still value me if I don't meet their goals?" And the more the Type A ponders these troubling questions, the more prone he becomes to the anxieties that have produced many unhappy hours in the Blondi family.

Performance anxiety explains what at first glance may seem a paradoxical finding: that studies show a significant subsection of Type A boys and girls who do poorly in school. Many Type A's perform badly because they're impatient, but many are also so anxious about living up to their Superachiever parent's high academic expectations that they freeze in test-taking situations. Alexi has such a problem with this that Joanne has been called in twice by his teacher for conferences.

The Superachiever's directiveness can foster another form of anxiety: disruptive acting out. Over time, the child's concerns about doing well in school spread to other areas of his behavior, and he tends to become like Alexi, whose noisy acting out in Cub Scouts last year made him such a disruptive influence that Joanne was asked to remove him from the group.

Parent-oriented communication is another aspect of the Superachiever style that can help promote negative Type A behavior. An example of this trait is the way Joanne responded when Alexi expressed a wish to cut back on his extracurricular activities. In addition to a Saturday morning karate class, these included a Tuesday afternoon gym class, a Wednesday after-school computer class, and a Thursday afternoon pottery class.

Before approaching Joanne with this request, Alexi had thought carefully about the reasons why he wanted to lighten his schedule: He felt he was under tremendous pressure, and he wanted more time to play. But he never got a chance to explain his reasons. As soon as he mentioned wanting to drop two classes, Joanne shook her head and said, "I know you're too young to understand, but these classes are important to your future. Mommy wouldn't have enrolled you in them if she didn't love you."

The link between parent-oriented communication and Type A behavior lies in the effect it can have on the child's already fragile self-esteem. Although it is unintentional, the parent who denies her child the right to express his opinions and views (whether she agrees with them or not) in effect tells him, "What you think and feel doesn't count." And this message (if it is consistently repeated, it's important to emphasize) produces one of two responses. Often, in non-Type A children, it leads to withdrawal. "Who needs you?" the spurned boy or girl thinks. But in the Type A, with his peculiar bundle of insecurities, it frequently has the opposite effect. Determined to show that he does count, the Type A strives harder and harder to give Mom and Dad the one thing he knows will make them feel he counts—successes and victories.

Another danger of parent-centered communication is that it often casts an unhappy shadow on the Type A's relationships with his friends. How a youngster communicates with those around him is, in large part, modeled on his communication with his parents. When that experience hasn't taught him to respect other people's thoughts and feelings, he'll emulate that lesson in his dealings with other children. What got the parents of the youngsters Alexi had excluded from his magic show so furious wasn't the exclusion itself, but that Alexi was so insensitive to the children's hurt and disappointment that when one of them began to cry, Alexi laughed at him.

After this incident, I told Joanne about the following five strategies I've developed to help Superachievers make their style work more effectively for themselves and their Type A's.

*Examine your success need.* This success need is the engine that drives the Superachiever. While understanding its origins won't automatically change the behaviors it produces, it will make them easier to control. Joanne's self-examination provides a case in point. As she began thinking about the roots of her success need, she found that in one way or another they all led back to the same source: her domineering, directive, perfectionistic Type A mother, Carol. This realization in turn led Joanne to a second discovery: how, as a child, she used to wilt when the full force of her mother's Type A personality was focused on her. "I could never show Mom a drawing or a book report without her immediately telling me how I could make it better," Joanne told me one day.

Remembering the anxiety and hurt her mother's words had produced hasn't made Joanne's directive impulse go away, but it has enhanced her control of it. Now, she's better able to visualize the impact her words of advice and instruction have on Alexi's fragile 7-year-old self.

*Appoint a monitor who can increase your awareness of your Superachiever impulses.* A finding from Dr. Bracke's study illustrates why this strategy is important. When Dr. Bracke asked the parents, "How often do you offer advice and instruction to your child?" all, in one way or another said, "When appropriate, but no more than other parents do." But when Dr. Bracke asked the Type A children of these parents the same question, all, in one way or another, said, "All Mom and Dad do is offer advice and instruction."

Were the Superachiever parents lying to Dr. Bracke?

No. It's simply that the traits which define the style are so deeply embedded in the Superachiever's psyche that she doesn't realize how often she uses them. The purpose of the monitor, who can be a spouse or a close friend or relative, is to help remind her by discreetly signaling whenever she begins to employ a social comparison or threatens to become overly helpful. If the impulse to use either of these traits proves uncontrollable, the monitor also can serve as a surrogate for the child. In practical terms, this means that the Superachiever asks the monitor, instead of the Type A, "How did your friend Billy do on the test?", or tells him, instead of the A, how to improve his homework or his tennis game.

There are also a number of things a parent can do on her own to control her Superachiever impulses. One simple technique is to physically distance herself from the Type A by going into another room when she feels an urge to compare or to correct him. Another, even better strategy is to write down her comparisons or instructions on paper. Besides providing an alternate source of expression, seeing how quickly her comparisons and advice fill up a sheet of paper can be a great consciousness-raiser.

*Provide "just being" time.* Sometimes the Superachiever's need to have an accomplished, successful child makes her lose sight of the vulnerable boy or girl beneath the Type A sheen of confidence. A case in point is a recent University of Michigan study by Sara Lee Cohen, who found that, compared to the other mothers in her study group, the Superachiever working mothers provided their children with far more educational and far fewer nurturing experiences.

The purpose of "just being" time is to right this balance. Holding, hugging, exchanging secrets, laughing at jokes, sharing confidences—these are the kinds of nurturing activities that produce love and joy in a child. The best way to ensure that the Type A gets his required share of them is to set aside a special time when parent and child don't do anything more important than be with and enjoy each other.

Since some Superachievers are uncomfortable with completely open-ended time, an activity can be added to give parent and child a medium for relating to each other. If you use this strategy, however, be careful not to fall into the trap Joanne fell into.

Three days after I suggested using cooking projects to focus her "just being" time, Joanne called and asked if I could recommend a lower-intensity activity. "Phillip says every time I go into the kitchen with Alexi, all he hears for the next hour is me telling Alexi what to do."

In such cases, the best strategy is to do what I suggested Joanne do: let Alexi select and lead the activities for a part of their relaxed time. Not only will this ensure that the things parent and child do together are things the Type A enjoys, but chances are he'll select games and activities he's good at, which will give him an opportunity to do what he's probably bursting to do: give his directive mother or father some direction.

*Use social comparisons carefully.* When employed indiscriminately, such comparisons can promote excessive achievement striving and anxiety. However, there are times when their use is not only appropriate but beneficial to the Type A.

One, for example, is in helping him gain perspective on a defeat. Placing thirtieth in a race, for example, becomes a lot more tolerable to a 12-year-old Type A when he's reminded that in a hundred-man field, thirtieth is a very respectable showing. Social comparison also can be used to promote some important personal values. For instance, pointing out to the Type A that while friend Jimmy may not be the soccer star he is, Jimmy's worked very hard to improve his game, is a way of reminding the A that some qualities—like perseverance and grit—are as important, if not more important, than being number one.

*Cut back on the Type A's early learning experiences.* In moderation, such experiences can be beneficial; they stimulate and challenge a child in ways that pay intellectual and emotional dividends. But an endless round of self-improvement classes—and by that I mean four or five per week—is bad for any child. As we shall see in chapter 5, it's an especially bad setup for a Type A because the pressures and stress often exacerbate his tendency toward anger, hostility, and impatience.

### Joe Cronin: The Critic

Two legends have dominated 9-year-old Billy Cronin's life. One centers on the October afternoon in 1975 when his father's fourth-quarter pass interception transformed a certain Army win into a last-minute Boston College upset. The other was Lieutenant Joe Cronin's rescue of a drowning fellow Marine on a June day three years later.

Grandfather Mike and grandmother Frances and mother Marge (but never Joe himself) have told and retold these stories dozens of times, and with each retelling their hero always grows a little more imposing in Billy's eyes.

The real-life Joe Cronin is nearly as impressive as the picture of him in his son's mind's eye. He is a big, rangy, handsome man with a Clint Eastwood squint, and the easy physical grace and confidence of a natural athlete who has seen ten thousand football fans leap to their feet to cheer him.

In his own way, Billy is just as impressive as his father. Tall and big-boned, with his mother's blond good looks and Joe's broad shoulders and athletic ability, he is a talented soccer player and a superb third baseman, as well as a good student with special aptitudes in math and art.

Billy is, in other words, everything you'd imagine a Type A child to be. Indeed, such is his aura of competence and energy that among his friends and peers, Billy is already the stuff of legends. Among his legion of admirers at the Sudbary elementary school, nothing is thought to be beyond Billy Cronin. Rumor even has it that last winter, when Billy announced that he wanted to go to Florida, Marge and Joe dropped everything to take him, and when he met the Yankees' second baseman Steve Sax at a recent baseball card show, Steve invited Billy to be his guest at a Yankee game.

Neither story is true, nor is it true that Billy's soccer tryout was taped by a TV news crew or that his weekly allowance is twenty dollars, but these tales are carefully cultivated by Billy, who carefully cultivates anything he thinks will give him an edge over his friends.

As much as Billy is admired, a certain wariness is also apparent in his peers' dealings with him. No one gets too close to him, because no one wants to run afoul of the angry Billy, who's been known to throw a punch at the slightest provocation. Nor do his friends want to compete with the hypercompetitive Billy, who doesn't think twice about bending the rules in his favor; or just relax with the hostile Billy, because they know sooner or later the very large chip on his shoulder will fall on their heads.

Marge Cronin is aware of her son's Type A traits, and she has a theory about their origins. She believes that, in one way or another, they all stem from Joe Cronin's frequent criticism of his son. "No matter how well Billy does," she told me the day she visited my office, "Joe always criticizes him for not doing better. He really expects Billy to be absolutely perfect."

Marge also has a theory about the origins of Joe's perfection need, and as I listened to her describe it, I realized I was hearing yet another example of that classic American story, the making of a Type A male.

Early on, Joe had been recognized as an outstanding student and athlete by his teachers, his coaches, and above all by his father. Mike Cronin was thrilled to have so talented a son, but like many fathers, Mike's delight at his good fortune quickly escalated into an expectation of perfection. Joe shouldn't just be a good student and athlete, he should be a perfect one. But, since perfection is a goal no boy can achieve, Joe spent a lot of his childhood wondering what Billy spends a lot of time wondering now: "Will anything I ever do please Dad?" Even the afternoon of his game-winning interception, Mike Cronin prefaced his congratulations to Joe by criticizing him for a fumble he made in the second quarter.

Marge, who told me this story during her visit, also told me she was certain that Billy's current problems arose from a recycling of this critical parental habit through another generation of Cronins. "I think a lot of Billy's fierce drive to win and his supercompetitiveness come from his desire to please Joe," she said, "and I think a lot of his anger comes from the frustration of knowing, no matter how hard he tries, he'll never succeed. I love my husband, Dr. Shelov, but if I were nine years old, I'd find him pretty intimidating."

This feeling, as well as Billy Cronin's pronounced anger, hypercompetitiveness, and achievement striving, is common among the Type A sons of men who develop Joe Cronin's parenting style. Billy's problem with truthfulness also is not uncommon among such boys. I call Joe's style "the Critic" and its practitioners, like him, often are successful middle- and upper-middle-class men, whose normal vulnerability to the Type A effect is increased by their high personal-achievement needs, and even more by the presence of an energetic, intelligent, athletically inclined, seemingly self-confident Type A son. Like Joe, under the effect's sway, these fathers form the sky-high goal that such a wonderful child should be perfect, and often, being men, they transmit this goal through the very male trait of criticism.

Of the three characteristics that define the style, the most pronounced is the one that gives it its name. No matter how good a son's performance, the Critic's use of criticism will leave the child feeling that, "Dad had something a little more perfect in mind." A case in point is the behavior of the Critic dads who took part in a study by researchers Wendy Kliewer of the University of California and Gerdi Weidner of the State University of New York. In all performance tasks (such as puzzle assembly), the investigators found that the Type A sons of Critic fathers outperformed their Type B counterparts, often by a wide margin. But since, like Billy, none of the A's performed as perfectly as their Critic fathers expected, instead of winning praise they were criticized.

*Authoritarian discipline.* This is the second major characteristic of the critic. Simply put, it means invoking paternal authority rather than reason in disciplining situations. In other words, a Critic won't explain why a transgression is wrong, but will fall back on power assertions ("Don't do that!") or authority ("It's wrong because I say it's wrong!") in condemning a behavior.

*Competitive-oriented value system.* This is another characteristic of the Critic. Like goals, a child's values are shaped by his family, and while a competitive-oriented value system is common in Type A families generally, being men and often being high Type A's, Critics are especially prone to pass on to their sons a value system that defines success largely—and sometimes exclusively—in terms of rank and status. On the day Joe got his new 500 class Mercedes, he and Billy spent an hour cruising the neighborhood, then came back and announced to Marge that theirs was the only one within a six-block radius.

Women often are dismayed and baffled by the Critic's style. Why would a parent be so harsh? they wonder. Many men, however, not only find the style familiar—after all, criticism and competition have an honored place in the male rite of passage—but they have a soft spot for it, because they know what's really going on beneath the criticism. In his own awkward way, Dad is saying to his son, "I love you so much I want you to be perfect."

Like all parenting styles, the Critic's possesses some important strengths. One is that it can help shape a child's own critical skills—and frequently in ways that delight a youngster. Joe Cronin's running commentaries of the baseball and football games he and Billy watch are an example. Like most Critics, Joe can't watch a sporting event without pointing out why quarterback A is so inept or second baseman B so good, and the knowledge his criticism transmits teaches Billy about more than sports. It also teaches him how to objectively and honestly identify and evaluate mistakes—his own and other people's.

Watch the expression on Billy's face as he listens to Joe's sports commentaries, and a second important asset of the Critic's style becomes apparent: it's a good vehicle for father-son bonding. Joe's running critiques give him and Billy what Marge's hugs and kisses give her and Moria, the Cronins' younger daughter: a medium for relating that is appropriate to their sensibilities.

When Joe's critical eye turns from an inept quarterback to Billy himself, however, his style becomes an active agent in his son's negative Type A behavior. An example was Joe's reaction to a drawing of GI Joe Billy did recently. Drawing military superheroes is something of a Cronin family tradition. Just as Billy does now, Joe spent hours as a boy copying and recopying pictures from his favorite war comic books.

Marge has some reservations about this particular Cronin tradition. But she's kept them to herself because Billy's drawings are one of the few things that earn Joe's unqualified praise—or rather earned, since recently Billy's artwork also has come under attack. "I don't know whether it's because Billy's getting older and Joe feels he can be more demanding, or Joe's just getting more demanding, period," Marge said during her visit. "But lately Billy's pictures have been getting the same reception as everything else he does."

To illustrate her point, she told me the story of the GI Joe drawing:

"It was a neat little picture, I really liked it. But Joe couldn't find one nice thing to say about it. He even criticized the color of the sky. Billy didn't say anything. He just kept nodding his head. But the next day, when I was putting fresh underwear in his dresser, I found the picture at the bottom of one of his drawers. It was torn to shreds."

In any child, behavior like Joe's would produce anger. And, since unrelenting parental criticism is a form of sky-high goal-setting because it says "success is what you haven't achieved yet," Joe's behavior also produces hypercompetitiveness and achievement striving. But there are some special reasons why the Critics' sons score very high on these two Type A traits. One is the unique nature of the Type A father–Type A son connection. While boys (including Type A boys) see disappointing Mom as an occupational hazard of being a son, disappointing Dad (especially when Dad is a powerful, successful, self-assured Type A) is such a frightening prospect that a Type A son will push himself furiously to be the perfect son his father wants him to be.

The other reason why a great degree of hypercompetitiveness and achievement striving is so common in boys like Billy is the Critic's value system. If Dad, who represents all that is glamorous and powerful in the world, defines his success only by the size of his salary or house or job title or the make of his car, in time the son will develop his competitive mindset and the characteristics that go along with it.

For example, Billy Cronin can tell you the amount of each of his friends' allowances, the number of rooms in their houses, how big—or small—their parents' cars are, roughly what they cost, and which families in the neighborhood own the most things. Billy also can tell you *exactly* where he and the Cronin family stand in all of these various ratings.

Billy's competitive mindset is directed at his family, as well. When cousin Jeffrey visited from Illinois last year, Billy spent their first hour together telling Jeffrey all the reasons why New York State was bigger and better than Illinois.

One effect of such "I'm better than you" behavior is that it always puts the child in opposition, even to his friends. Thirty years from now, the mindset behind this behavior will add to Billy Cronin's risk of incurring heart disease because it will cut him off from the most effective antidote to the Type A cardiac risk: the love and appreciation of others.

This cardiac risk arises from another Type A trait that Critics' sons score high on—anger. Often, by age 11 or 12, the failure to live up to Dad's perfectionism has produced so much anger in a Critic's son that he begins displaying high-for-his-age cholesterol and blood pressure levels. The wariness even close friends show toward Billy, and some of the troubling things the parents of those friends say about him, illustrate how much of this anger accumulates in a Critic's son by age 9. So, too, does the dinnertime explosion that prompted Marge Cronin's visit to me.

The day of the blowup, Billy had made a serious error in a Little League game. At dinner, when Joe brought up the error, it was with the intention of being sympathetic and supportive. But, like many Critics' sons, Billy had become so conditioned to parental criticism that when Joe said, "That was a nice try this morning," Billy heard, "You blew it again." His response to that imagined criticism was immediate and sharp.

"You don't care about me; you never have!" Billy said, leaping up from his chair, "Well, I hate you, you hear me? I hate you!"

Joe's style is linked to another behavior of Billy's that is sometimes seen in Critics' sons. Marge didn't mention it, however, until near the end of our talk, and then only with reluctance. We'd been discussing Billy's behavior at school, when suddenly she turned to the window.

"There's one thing I haven't told you, Dr. Shelov. Billy's been accused of cheating."

Marge explained that the problem first came to light two

years ago, when a playmate complained to her that Billy had cheated in a game. At the time, Marge was inclined to dismiss the accusation as sour grapes. But several months later, when the mother of another friend mentioned a cheating incident involving Billy, Marge grew concerned, and when Billy's teacher called her in to discuss his questionable behavior on an English test, her concern turned into outright alarm.

While this kind of moral corner-cutting reflects the child's deep desire to please Dad by producing victory after victory, it originates in the Critic's authoritarian discipline style.

Children don't come into the world with a clear sense of right and wrong; it has to be taught to them. And while parental discipline can be a very effective teaching tool, a discipline style that condemns misbehaviors solely because they displease Dad, and chooses punishments solely because they satisfy Dad's anger, teaches a child nothing about right and wrong. It simply teaches him what Dad doesn't like and what may happen to him if he displeases Dad. While this often makes the child the world's leading authority on Dad's dislikes, it doesn't teach the kind of moral reasoning that can be fostered when a parent takes the time to explain why a misbehavior is wrong and reprimands the child in a way that forces him to think through the logical consequences of his misdeed. In time, these measures help a youngster to think about his behavior's effect on others. In the most elemental sense, this is what moral reasoning means.

Much as he may want to win, the Type A who develops moral reasoning will, in competitive situations, stop and think: "I want to win, but it would be unfair to others to win by cheating." The Type A who can't reason in this way will, in competitive situations, think what Billy Cronin usually does: "How can I win, period?"

How can the Critic make his style work more effectively for his Type A?

During a visit to my office, I told Joe Cronin I'd found four strategies to be particularly effective in helping Critic fathers like himself. They are:

*Examine your perfection need.* Just as asking, "Where does my success need originate?" can help the Superachiever gain an insight into the impulse that drives her style, asking, "Where does my perfection need originate?" can help the Critic gain an insight into the need that drives his style. But in his case, one caveat should be imposed on this form of self-scrutiny. Being a male, he may not be as comfortable with the process of self-examination as is the Superachiever, who is often a woman. (Men can be Superachievers too.) One way to resolve this difficulty is by following a suggestion I made to the Cronins: Have Marge serve as sounding board and guide for the exploration. I knew she had enough knowledge of her Critic husband to help him explore his perfection need in depth, and enough sensitivity to ensure that the exploration wouldn't be so probing that it became daunting.

*Reduce criticism.* One method of implementing this strategy is by thinking of the child's age and development stage when the impulse to find fault arises. Disappointing as a 9-year-old's missed catch can be, the temptation to criticize it all but disappears if a father reminds himself that a 9-year-old's still-immature nervous system makes such flubs inevitable. The same is true for the 7-year-old's misplaced umbrella and the 6-year-old's lost gloves. These errors become very forgivable if the Critic knows that such forgetfulness is age-appropriate behavior for a first- or second-grader.

Reminding himself of how he felt when his father—or mother or teacher—criticized him also can help the Critic put a cap on his critical impulse. Remembering how humiliated and frightened he felt when his father criticized him helped Joe Cronin realize that what Billy heard in his critical words wasn't his intended message—"I love you so much I want you to be perfect"—but rather, the one he used to hear in his father's criticisms: "You're inadequate, you're unworthy, you don't measure up."

Later, Marge told me that of all the strategies I had suggested to Joe, this one had the most dramatic effect.

*Create a more three-dimensional picture of yourself in the child's mind.* If Critic fathers tend to have a one-dimensional view of their Type A sons (being perfect), those sons often have an equally one-dimensional view of their fathers: that of a fault-finder. This explains why the Critic father/Type A son relationship tends to be narrow and confining. Because Dad's behavior makes the child think of him in one role only—that of

Critic—when the youngster is looking for someone to fill the other roles in his life (such as adviser, friend, confidant, companion on an overnight camping trip or Saturday afternoon baseball game), the last person in the world he thinks of is Dad.

During one of his visits, I told Joe Cronin that if he hoped to make himself a candidate for these other, more important (and more satisfying) roles, he'd have to encourage Billy to think of him in a more three-dimensional way. I explained that there were two methods he could use to do that. One was by asking Marge to take over a greater share of the disciplining, chore overseeing, and other parental responsibilities that are likely to put a mother or father into conflict with a child. "No matter what else you do with Billy," I said, "he'll continue to think of you the way he does now if you have to keep reminding him to pick up his room or do his homework. But since Marge can say these things without fear of being stereotyped, let her serve as Billy's taskmaster for a while."

Critics like Joe also can become less critical by increasing (or inaugurating) father-son "just being" time. Humor, a knack for storytelling, an encyclopedic knowledge of dinosaurs or the 1937 New York Yankees—the Critic has all the talents and knowledge you'd expect an intelligent, well-informed man to possess. And "just being" time gives his son an opportunity to discover these new (and, very likely, unexpected) sides of Dad. Some sort of activity is needed to give structure to this time, but, as in the Superachiever's case, it should be a low-key one that doesn't overshadow the principal purpose of just being together—relating and discovering—and isn't likely to trigger the father's propensity to criticize. One can choose an activity in which the son is in charge and the father can ask questions and make positive comments.

*Adopt a new disciplinary style.* In chapter 10 we'll take a look at the respect-oriented disciplinary style and why it fosters a firm sense of right and wrong in Type A boys and girls. Suffice it to say here that the parent who employs an authoritarian disciplining style helps to promote the kind of moral myopia that can condemn his Type A to a lifetime of problems.

### Rebecca Little: The Hurrier

Some days Rebecca Little feels she doesn't have a single dream left. Her biggest one, the dream that brought her to New York twenty years ago, was to be an actress. Just as her high school yearbook predicted, Rebecca intended to be "Nashville's gift to Broadway." That dream died a long, slow death, the victim of an endless grind of casting calls and rejections. But out of it, a new one took shape.

In 1977, at an audition for *Jesus Christ Superstar,* Rebecca found herself sitting next to a dark-haired, sharp-featured young man named Bruce Gilbert. Nine months later, she was married to Bruce, working in the fragrances department of Bloomingdale's, and dreaming a new dream: the family they would share once Bruce established himself as an actor. That dream died too; six years later, on a Greenwich Village street, Bruce hugged Rebecca and their two children goodbye and stepped into a cab, headed to the airport for a flight to Los Angeles.

Their separation was supposed to be temporary—Bruce was to send for the family once he'd established himself in television—but Rebecca wasn't entirely surprised when it ended in divorce two years later. Nor has it entirely surprised her that, in the years since, financial responsibility for raising their two children has fallen largely on her shoulders.

When I met Rebecca, the elder of those youngsters was 10. Her name is Anna, and she is 13 now. On Rebecca's blue days, when she is trying to think of things that will cheer her up, usually the first thing that comes to mind is Anna.

"Anna is everything I'm not," she told me one day not long after I'd become the family's pediatrician. As I got to know mother and daughter, I came to understand what Rebecca meant. While her mother is mercurial, tentative, ethereal, and slightly scattered—in the way that overburdened people often are—Anna is concrete, practical, deliberate, and, above all, competent.

Anna is also a Type A, but, like Alexi Blondi, she represents a variation on the classic A pattern. In terms of her personality, she is a quiet, almost somber child. In fact, her only noticeable Type A trait is her competence, but it is so palpable and all-embracing that it has made her the center of emotional gravity in the family.

Rebecca relies on Anna in ways I think she doesn't even realize, while younger brother Jason looks to Anna for the nurturance and stability his mercurial mother is sometimes unable to provide. If Jason hurts himself or wants advice or someone to arrange a play date, he turns first to his big sister.

Outwardly, Anna appears to have borne the pressures and responsibilities thrust on her with remarkable equanimity. Unlike many other Type A's, whose high-strung temperament often leads them to act out stresses in angry, hostile, and impatient behavior, Anna is always a model of calmness and self-possession. But in her own quiet way she has paid a price for the responsibilities she bears. In Type A's who, like Anna, internalize rather than externalize their anxieties and stresses, frequently the behavior pattern creates a vulnerability to depression and somatic complaints like headaches and stomachaches.

This form of Type A behavior, with its depressive and psychosomatic components, is common among the children of parents who share Rebecca's parenting style. I call this style the "Hurrier," and its practitioners tend to be like Rebecca—overburdened working mothers (especially single working mothers), whose normal vulnerability to the Type A effect is enhanced by the lack of an adult support system to rely on for comfort and relief. The absence of such a system also plays a key role in shaping the sky-high goals that Hurriers form for their children. Tufts University psychologist David Elkind describes the general sky-high goal as "adultification." Simply put, adultification means the tendency to push a child to develop adultlike emotional and psychological competencies; in his book *The Hurried Child*, Dr. Elkind declares it to be an important cause of negative Type A behavior in children.

Of the Hurrier style's two main traits, the most pronounced is *delegation*. Being overburdened, Hurriers assign more and weightier chores to their children than do other parents, and they do so at an earlier age. Rebecca is a case in point. Although Anna is only 13, she is responsible for picking up Jason after school, looking after him until Rebecca arrives home, shopping, making the family dinner, and, on nights when Rebecca's too tired to do it herself, putting Jason to bed.

*Openness* is the style's other main characteristic, and one of the ways Hurriers express it is in a willingness to expose themselves—their hopes and dreams and fears—to their children in unusually adult, intimate ways. Rebecca's conversations with Anna about Adam, her male friend, and about the family's financial problems are examples of this kind of openness. Rebecca's willingness to let her children follow their own developmental paths is an example of a second kind of Hurrier openness: a tolerance and acceptance of a child's individuality.

This trait also constitutes one of the style's chief strengths, and in Rebecca's home, its principal beneficiary has been Anna's younger brother, Jason. Quiet, thoughtful, bookish boys like Jason are a source of consternation and concern to many parents. Young males are supposed to like baseball, not books, and when this stereotype is resisted, frequently there is much friction between parent and child. However, Jason has been left free to march to the beat of his own drum, and someday, when he's old enough to know how unusual such freedom is, he will realize how lucky he was to have a parent as open and accepting as Rebecca.

Anna's wisdom and steadiness illustrate another asset of the Hurrier style. Within certain limits, Rebecca's delegation of responsibility for the care of a younger sibling and for household chores helps to develop the qualities that have made Anna such an impressive child to her teachers and the parents of her friends. Mature and dependable, she is that rarest of creatures, a youngster on the verge of adolescence who can always be trusted to do what she says and do it properly.

There are times, though, when Rebecca's Hurrier style actively promotes Anna's vulnerability to Type A. An example was her behavior following a long, stormy phone conversation with her friend Adam.

Rebecca's relationship with Adam, which began about a year ago, is a troubled one. And, given her penchant for openness, she keeps Anna thoroughly appraised of these troubles. On this particular night, as soon as she got off the phone, she told Anna about Adam's threat to stop seeing her if she didn't lend him three thousand dollars. Then she burst into tears.

Later that night, still feeling drained by the conversation, Rebecca displayed another Hurrier trait—delegation. She asked Anna to read Jason his good-night story and put him to bed.

Rebecca's responses in both instances was Type A-behavior–producing for the same reason. In asking Anna to provide her with adultlike comfort and support and Jason with adultlike nurturance, she was telling her daughter, "Mommy expects you to act like a grownup." Frequently this message sets off its own kind of Type A achievement striving. Except in this case, the achievement being strived for isn't a win or a victory, but to be the adultlike tower of strength that Mother expects her child to be. More often than not, in time, the child who's encouraged to pursue this goal begins to chase after new responsibilities and chores the way other A's chase after new victories and wins. And often this form of achievement striving ends up boomeranging on the Type A in the form of minor psychosomatic ailments.

It wasn't coincidence that the morning following Adam's phone call, Anna awoke with a stomachache. Nor was it coincidence that a month earlier, following a discussion with Rebecca about the family's perilous financial condition, Anna developed a blinding headache.

Depression also is common in the Type A children of Hurriers, and in Anna's case, it has produced a heartbreaking result. Unlike other girls her age, whose lives are a brightly lit whirl of parties and dances, Anna's life is gray and monochromatic. When she isn't serving Rebecca or Jason, she spends most of her time alone in her bedroom, munching cookies and switching the TV aimlessly from channel to channel.

How can Anna be helped?

When Rebecca put that question to me, I told her about four strategies I've found to be especially effective in making the Hurrier's style work more effectively for the Hurrier and her Type A.

They are:

*Create a support group for yourself.* This is the foundation of any lasting change in the Hurrier's style. All of us occasionally need a shoulder to lean on, and if there aren't any adult shoulders available, whether we intend to or not, we end up leaning on a child's—particularly if he or she looks as strong and self-assured as Anna does.

But where can the often isolated Hurrier find available adult shoulders?

One good source are her parents, but let me add one cautionary note. For this strategy to work, the comfort level between the Hurrier and her parents has to be such that she can talk freely about the most intimate details of her life without fear of parental reproach or condemnation.

Another source of available adult shoulders are friends and co-workers. Single working mothers often are willing to give support and comfort to other single working mothers. A third source are single-parent support groups. Information about such groups can be obtained from pediatricians, local churches and synagogues, hospitals, and so on.

*Make the child feel like a child again.* It's a truism, but an important one: All children come into the world biologically programmed to expect nurturance and love. When at the age of 8 or 10 or 15 they find themselves instead called on to nurture and comfort an adult parent, negative Type A behavior is only one of many potentially damaging consequences that may arise. The goal of this strategy is to restore parent and child to their appropriate roles, and it can be implemented in three ways.

One is by making the child's—not the parent's—needs, fears, anxieties, and uncertainties the focus of the parent-child dialogue. You'll learn how to do this in detail in chapter 9. Suffice it to say here that the parent who develops this ability not only gives her child the attention and nurturance he expects, he or she also gives him an opportunity to voice emotions, which, unvoiced, can lead to depression and somatization.

Pampering, in the form of preparing a favorite dinner, declaring a chore-free Saturday, or fussing over an accomplishment, is another way to restore the parent-child relationship to its rightful balance.

A third way is to reduce the youngster's adultlike responsibilities. I realize that the realities of time and money make chores necessary in most Hurrier homes. But a Hurrier parent should make a special effort to avoid casting an older sibling in the role of principal nurturer for a younger one. This isn't to say an 11-, 12-, or 13-year-old can't babysit, put Band-Aids on cuts, or occasionally act as an adviser to a younger sibling. What he or she can't do, however, is serve as a major source of comfort, understanding, and nurturance for that sibling, and when he or she is put in the position of having to try, everyone suffers.

*Build a support system for the child.* Work and other responsibilities often make the Hurrier unavailable to her child at special moments, such as a debut at a school play or an emotional crisis brought on by a thoughtless peer's remarks. The purpose of building a support system, whose members can include grandparents, aunts, uncles, a special teacher, or other special adults, is to provide the child with figures who can act as parental surrogates at such important moments. Uncle Joe and Aunt Bea aren't Mom or Dad, but knowing they are available to lend support makes stressful moments a lot easier for a child.

*Be nice to yourself.* Rebecca thought I was speaking tongue-in-cheek when I told her I thought it was also important for her to start being a better friend to herself. But the fact is, a little enlightened selfishness—whether it takes the form of an afternoon aerobics class or an after-work drink date or a Sunday afternoon bike ride—is essential to maintaining the vitality and zest every parent, and especially a single parent, needs to be an exciting, stimulating companion to a child.

I also told Rebecca that such acts of enlightened selfishness would become particularly important if she noticed herself succumbing to the signs of emotional and spiritual exhaustion, such as inattentiveness to her physical appearance and a loss of interest in activities that normally pleased her. "Being a good friend to yourself," I told her, "will make you a better mother to Anna and Jason."

# 4

# Iron Man and King of the Hill: The Type A and Significant Others

Parents aren't the only ones who notice the Type A's unusual energy, drive, and ambition. Teachers, coaches, caregivers, and even peers find them just as eye-catching. And sometimes the result can be immensely beneficial for the Type A.

Lisa McCain, an 11-year-old patient of mine, offers a case in point. Last year, Lisa's motivation and disciplined study habits won her so much extra teacher time and attention that this year, she was one of a half-dozen seventh-graders at her school selected to take the SATs. And 6-year-old Jeremy Bender's unusually rich relationship with his caregiver, Dothlyn, has its starting point in Dothlyn's perception of him as an unusually exciting, intelligent, interesting child.

Sometimes, however, the Type A's aura of competence and authority elicits more problematic responses from his teachers, coaches, caregivers, and peers. The syndromes in this chapter offer some graphic examples. There are fourteen, and they grow out of my clinical observations. After the encounter with the critical caregiver I mentioned in chapter 2, I began wondering: Do significant others generally respond to Type A boys and girls in ways that are uniform enough to constitute distinct behavior patterns?

My observations not only indicated that they do, but that the patterns which characterize each group's relationship with the Type A also are distinct. As with parents, some are set in motion by overencouragement, others by hypercriticism, and still others by a demand for emotional competence that is beyond the Type A's maturity.

The patterns do share two characteristics. One is that in nearly every instance they are triggered by good intentions: the teacher, coach, or caregiver is simply trying to help the Type A realize his potential. The other is that all require prompt parental intervention, because while a coach's or a teacher's criticism or pushiness won't turn a positive Type A into a negative one, such behavior can markedly exacerbate a preexisting tendency toward negative Type A behavior.

Although these Type A–fostering syndromes represent this chapter's major focus, I've included several other patterns that parents should be aware of because of the more general risks they pose for the Type A child. For the most part, the patterns in this latter group arise from the underside of the Type A effect. Besides being eye-catchingly bright, motivated, and ambitious, Type A's can be contentious, challenging and abrasive. These behaviors can put a serious strain on the Type A's relationships with others.

Here's how both types of behavior patterns arise.


TEACHERS

A recent Colgate University study explains why teachers respond so enthusiastically to their Type A pupils.

Colgate psychologists Anna Fontana and John Davido report that, compared to other students, Type A's spend more time on homework, focus better in the classroom, win more academic honors, and are so motivated that the stresses that normally disrupt a child's classroom performance—such as a fight with a parent or girl- or boyfriend—don't disrupt theirs. Four of the five syndromes that characterize teacher–Type A relations arise from the sky-high expectations this academically assured child inspires.

### The Iron Man

The Iron Man's behavior pattern originates in the expectation that the directed, motivated Type A student will be invulnerable to the stresses that affect other students. This expectation is problematic because when the Type A doesn't live up to it, the teacher misinterprets the reason. Instead of thinking, "This able student isn't doing well. Maybe he has a problem I can help him with," the teacher thinks, "This able student is goofing off. I'd better get on his case." Exhibit A of the phenomenon is a teacher I'll call Mr. Hartford.

Normally, seventh-grade teachers like Mr. Hartford are very sensitive to the problems that accompany the transition from grammar school to junior high. There are so many new challenges and anxieties that frequently a student's grades take a temporary drop. But last year, when the grades of Danny Langone, one of my 13-year-old Type A's, took such a drop, Mr. Hartford momentarily lost his sensitivity. Danny looked so competent and self-assured, Mr. Hartford was convinced that his disappointing academic performance was due to laziness. So, instead of trying to help ease Danny's adjustment to junior high, Mr. Hartford got on his case in a very public way.

By the fifth week of school he had dubbed Danny "the lethargic Mr. Langone," and by the eighth week his public and private rebukes had produced such pressure that a crack developed in Danny's Iron Man facade.

One morning just before Thanksgiving break, Danny made a snowball and flung it at one of his classmates, breaking the boy's glasses and injuring his eye seriously enough to require a visit to the ophthalmologist.

This kind of angry, out-of-character acting out (Danny had never been involved in such an incident before) is, along with regressive behavior, a chief Iron Man trait. It is also a chief danger, since the more often a teacher expresses his sky-high expectations of invulnerability, the angrier the A becomes at being pressured so relentlessly.

Should your child develop these symptoms, there are two things to do. The first is speak to his teacher. You can't always count on a busy, overworked teacher to spot your A's problems, but you can almost always count on his goodwill. Often, just explaining why your Type A is upset will bring a stop to the pressuring.

You should also devise ways to help your Type A cope with the stress that's throwing him off pace. A good example of how this technique works is the way Maria Langone used it to ease Danny's adjustment difficulties. One of Maria's best inspirations was to institute a daily preschool briefing. Each morning at breakfast, Danny would describe the situations and events he was most worried about that day. Then, Maria would suggest things he could do to make them less anxiety-provoking. For example, when Danny said he was worried about sitting alone at lunch, Maria recommended he make a lunch date as soon as he got to school, and when he voiced concern about a history test, she suggested he sit next to a friend during the test. These strategies provided Danny with the support he needed to ease his anxieties.

### Survival of the Fittest

Like Iron Man, this behavior also arises out of a common teacher expectation about Type A's. Believing that Type A's can tolerate very high levels of competition, and indeed that they thrive on it, often a teacher who finds himself with a classroom full of bright, aggressive A's will try to cultivate a Darwinian classroom atmosphere by encouraging his gifted, achievement-minded pupils to vie with one another for grades, praise, and teacher time and attention.

One of my 11-year-old A's, Barbara Furakawa, has a science teacher who is a good example of the type. I'll call him Mr. Wilson, and he prizes competition so much that when he announced the class's science fair, he also announced that the student who turned in the longest and most detailed report would win a pizza party for six, and two tickets to any movie of his or her choice.

Jan Furakawa, Barbara's mother, was very much of two minds about Mr. Wilson's methods. While she knew that a certain amount of competition is a healthy stimulant to learning, she also knew that a Type A child's ability to tolerate competition is limited. She knew as well that once a Type A is pushed past that limit by a too-competitive-minded teacher, trouble is likely to develop, in the form of an out-of-control achievement drive. And so it proved to be in her daughter's case. In the seven weeks leading up to the science fair, when Barbara wasn't in her room compiling what turned out to be an 80-page paper on microorganisms, she was on the phone tracking her classmates' progress.

When the fair finally opened, Jan discovered that her daughter wasn't the only Type A in the class whose achievement impulse had been set on fast-forward by the competitive-minded Mr. Wilson. Six other classmates had turned in reports of 80 pages or more. One unfortunate boy had actually done a 140-page report.

The excessive amount of time Barbara spent on her report, her preoccupation with her classmates' progress, and her disinterest in her friends and family—and all the other things 11-year-olds normally are interested in—are signs that a Type A has fallen victim to Survival of the Fittest behavior. The best way to extricate your child from it is to follow my advice to Barbara Furakawa.

Tell the teacher you're worried about the amount of time your child spends on homework and ask him: "Could you please speak to my child? I've asked him several times not to push himself too hard, but he won't listen to me." This technique worked very well with Mr. Wilson, who, like most teachers, was experienced enough at reading between the lines of parental messages to know what he was really being told: "Please lighten my child's workload." If this method doesn't work—and it won't with all competitive-minded teachers—then talk to the parents of your child's classmates. If they are as unhappy about the teacher's methods as you are, maybe a parental group can be formed to lobby for a less competitive classroom atmosphere.

### Who's the Boss?

Some teacher-student combinations are so perfect that divine intervention seems to have arranged them; others represent such a mismatch of styles and temperaments that the shadowy hand of the devil can almost be seen at work. "Who's the Boss?" arises from one such unhappy combination. Its partners are a cocky, high-spirited, verbally challenging Type A and a young, inexperienced teacher. The pattern is set in motion by a misperception about the origins of the Type A's behavior.

The high-spirited A is trying to show the teacher and his classmates how smart he is. But the teacher's inexperience and insecurity make him interpret the child's brash behavior as an expression of rebellion, and more often than not he responds by resolving to make the rebel an example, which he does either by freezing him out of classroom activities and discussions, by baiting him, or by publicly humiliating him when he asks a question or makes a mistake.

Sharp increases in anger and anxiety are one sign that a child has gotten caught up in "Who's the Boss?" behavior. Another, more specific sign is frequent complaints about the teacher. The Type A, who often appears glum and a little frightened, will complain that the teacher picks on him or corrects everything he says or makes fun of him in front of the rest of the class.

Obviously, a parent-teacher conference is imperative in such cases. But unless you're willing to acknowledge the teacher's concerns, it won't be productive. If your Type A is—as many are—sometimes cocky and abrasive, admit it. But also point out to the teacher what he or she probably doesn't know—that these behaviors arise from your child's desire to be perceived as a good student, rather than from mean-spiritedness. It's a good idea to follow this initial visit with a second one, this time including the child. One of the greatest promoters of mutual understanding and respect between adversaries is conversation in which each can explore the other's perception of their shared problem.

One word of warning: If, despite your best efforts, you sense that the teacher's view of your Type A remains unchanged, don't be afraid to tell the child, "This teacher won't let you get away with anything." Some parents may view this as bad-mouthing a teacher, but I think it might more accurately be described as an exercise in realpolitik. The child who is so cautioned will, out of self-protection, almost always modulate his behavior accordingly.

### You're My Star

This pattern occurs when a Type A child with the star qualities of energy, intelligence, and charisma meets a teacher who has a weakness for star-making. We've all encountered such teachers in our academic careers. They tend to behave a lot like a music teacher I'll call Mrs. Graham, whose designated stars would find themselves invited to nights at the opera, offered extra lessons after school, selected to represent the class at various school-wide events, and held up to other students as paragons of competence, diligence, and good behavior.

Last year, when Jimmy Poppopolus, one of my 16-year-old A's, was swept into Mrs. Graham's spotlight, he was deeply pleased—at least, at first. But, as Jimmy discovered, Mrs. Graham's stars aren't ever allowed to get a C or a C-minus, say or do a dumb thing, or show their hurts and disappointments. His pleasure quickly turned to unhappiness. As it did, his behavior at home (but not in Mrs. Graham's class, where he remained a model student) turned troublesome and, at times, baffling.

In addition to free-floating anger and anxiety, Jimmy developed a resistance to performing the simplest chores, and would sulk the moment the slightest thing went wrong or if asked to do something he considered beneath him. The day Theresa Poppololus described these symptoms to me, I told her they had two sources. Jimmy's free-floating anger and anxiety were by-products of Mrs. Graham's sky-high expectations, and his sulky, uppity attitude was linked to his star status. If he was treated as a special child at school, why shouldn't he be treated as one at home?

Along with these symptoms, other indications that a Type A has attained star status at school include an obsession with schoolwork, with the star-making teacher, and with the special school events in which he is participating. Explaining to the teacher the high toll stardom is taking on your child is the best way to extricate a Type A from this pattern. Just be sure that the extrication isn't abrupt, total, and, most important, done without the A's foreknowledge. He should be told, preferably by the teacher, what is about to happen and why. During the transition, you can make things easier on the star if you increase the time he spends in your spotlight.

### Stop Being Disruptive

If any child looks like a model of good classroom deportment, it is the composed, self-assured Type A. But sitting, waiting—all the things other children can do easily—often produce impatient, antsy behavior in the easily frustrated A. The Stop Being Disruptive pattern arises from the misdiagnosis that this contradiction encourages. Instead of seeing the A's deportment problems as by-products of a high-strung temperament, the teacher sees them as manifestations of the child's desire to be a troublemaker, and concludes that the best way to deal with him is to administer a strong dose of discipline.

The frequent warnings and visits to the detention room that follow are one sign that a Type A is involved in a Stop Being Disruptive behavior pattern. Another is a note from the teacher requesting an immediate conference with the parents. As with Who's the Boss?, the best way to make sure the conference is productive is to avoid being defensive. If your child's impatience sometimes makes him a behavior problem at home, chances are they also make him one in the classroom. Just be sure the teacher understands the true source of these problems.

During your visit, you might also mention that there are a number of things the teacher can do to eliminate the situations that provoke the negative behavior; for example, one simple way to eliminate a lot of the frustration produced by a raised hand that is not acknowledged is by telling the child he'll be called on as soon as classmate Tommy's question is answered. Still more frustration is eliminated if the Type A is given something to do while the teacher deals with Tommy.

### COACHES

While outstanding athletic ability isn't any more common among Type A boys and girls than it is among other children, as a group they possess an unusual abundance of other qualities that often are even more important to athletic success than is raw talent. These traits include competitive zest, leaderliness, and a fierce desire to win.

As a longtime Little League coach, I can attest to the sky-high expectations the owner of these qualities elicits in a coach's breast. Even if your Type A isn't particularly gifted athletically, because he's so determined, focused, and intelligent, often he'll be pressed into service as a team leader or motivator or on-field strategist.

The two syndromes that characterize Type A coach relations arise when this pressure becomes too intense.

### Do It for the Team

Its basic plot—the star athlete who, game after game, single-handedly carries the team to victory—is familiar from a dozen old movies. But its sandlot version differs from Hollywood's in two fundamental respects. Instead of a professional or at least college-age athlete, the star is usually an athletically gifted 8-, 10-, 12-, or 14-year-old Type A. Also, it never has a happy ending.

In a fairness to coaches, it should be pointed out that often they are as much victims of this pattern as Type A's, since the competitive nature of amateur athletics puts them under enormous pressure. Today, everyone from school officials, to Little League sponsors, to parents, to the players themselves, wants a winning team so badly, often the coach will do anything to produce such a team, even if doing anything means singling out one youngster and anointing him with responsibility for carrying the team to success.

How this responsibility is conveyed to the child varies from coach to coach, but in general the anointed A will find himself singled out for special praise, talked up among the parents of teammates, asked to coach less-able children, held up as a role model, and made into a confidant who is given special privy to the coach's hopes, dreams, and fears for the team. As with You're My Star, many aspects of Do It for the Team are deeply gratifying to the Type A's ego structure. It's nice to hear a special cheer each time you step up to the plate, hear your teammates warn opponents "Watch out" because you're on the team, nice to be applauded by their parents, and nicest of all to know you are the apple of your coach's eye.

But also as with You're My Star, over time the weight of these sky-high expectations begins to produce a notable sag in the star's shoulders. He begins to see each game as a series of bold anxiety-provoking question marks. Will he get that critical hit?

Will he be able to carry the team to victory this time?

One sign that a Type A has gotten caught up in Do It for the Team is the special attention he gets from the coach, his teammates, and their parents. Another sign is an increase in his tendency to criticize.

Sometimes the criticism will be directed at himself. He will criticize his single for not being a double and his double for not being a home run. At other times, it will be directed at his peers. Teammate Johnny will be criticized for his strikeout or teammate Tommy for his error. But in all cases, the criticism emanates from the same source: the terrible pressure the A feels to produce the victory everyone expects of him.

Increased achievement striving is another common manifestation of the syndrome. Again, as with You're My Star, the A develops an obsessive interest in honing his skills and an obsessive interest in tracking the progress of competing teams and their stars.

Generally, I make two recommendations to the parents of A's who get caught up in Do It for the Team. The first is to talk to the coach. If he's typical, there's a good chance that he won't be aware of the pressure under which he has put the child. Also, once he has been made aware of it, he'll probably begin spreading the responsibility for victory more evenly among the team. My other recommendation concerns the atypical coach. If, despite your request, the Type A continues to be saddled with responsibility for carrying the team, try to have him transferred. If that strategy fails or proves impractical (transfers are fairly common in Little League but impossible on school teams), remove him from the team. Even after you've carefully explained the reasons for your decision, your A won't be happy, but his unhappiness will pass. What might not pass are the hazards to which Do It for the Team exposes him.

### He Can Take It

During a recent Little League game, I had what was probably my thousandth encounter with He Can Take It, which is a very common problem afflicting Type A boys and girls. Annoyed by his star player's bungled attempt to steal home, the opposing coach leaped off the bench and, in front of me, the umpire, the parents, and the players, snapped at the boy, "Why did you do that, Tommy? Didn't you see my signal? I wanted you to hold at third!"

This kind of sharp, adult criticism is the chief feature of He Can Take It, and in its own (albeit backhanded) way, it's meant to be a compliment to the Type A. Because he seems so much more mature and more serious about bettering his performance than other youngsters his age, the coach feels he doesn't have to coddle him by modulating his criticism with praise for a "nice try" or "good effort," as coaches routinely do to protect their young players' fragile egos. With the Type A, he feels he can be direct, straightforward, and blunt, like the coach who snapped at Tommy.

In slightly different forms, this pattern also is common among the other adults around the Type A, including teachers and parents. The sky-high expectations that fuel it encompass more than expectations about the mature-seeming A's ability to absorb adult criticism. As Rebecca Little's story illustrates, it also frequently extends to the child's ability to absorb adult emotional and psychological information.

On the playing field, however, He Can Take It stands out in especially sharp relief. And while it rarely produces dramatic or sudden symptoms (unless, of course, the criticism is severe and unrelenting), because it gives the Type A one more reason to feel unvalued and unrespected (Why is the coach so mean about my mistakes?), it is sufficient cause for a parent-coach talk. As with Do It for the Team, often the coach won't be aware of the special way he's responding to the A, so frequently just bringing it to his attention will bring this behavior to an end.

### CAREGIVERS AND DAYCARE WORKERS

One of the most interesting findings to emerge from the caregiver–Type A study I mentioned in chapter 2 were the reasons that the overencouraging caregivers gave for their behavior.

As you might expect, many cited their charges' aura of competence (although, of course, none used that term), but a number of others cited an often overlooked aspect of the Type A effect: the Type A's burning desire to succeed. Because this desire, which is also expressed in a wish to appear competent and in control, is so palpable in even very young A's, understandably those around them often think, "How can you be too demanding or encouraging with a child who expects so much of himself?"

This attitude plays an important part in the Cheerleader, one of the most common Type A–caregiver patterns, and, to a lesser extent, in Do It Yourself, another common caregiver behavior. The Type A's sometimes prickly and abrasive personality plays an important part in control, as we'll see in the following pages.

### The Cheerleader

Commonly, this syndrome announces itself shortly after the arrival of the new caregiver, who is a Type B. Its chief warning signal is a notable increase in the toddler's or preschooler's negative Type A behavior. Suddenly the youngster, who previously had shown only occasional flashes of angry acting out and aggressive attention seeking, starts acting angry and seeking attention all the time. What links these troubling changes to the new Type B caregiver's arrival—and usually only to her arrival—is an odd bit of A/B chemistry that was highlighted in a recent study.

Looking at caregiver–Type A child interactions, the study's author found something surprising. Type B caregivers are unusually vulnerable to the Type A effect in that they push and encourage their Type A charges more than Type A caregivers do. The reason for this vulnerability remains unclear. My feeling is that it's a form of compensatory behavior; eager to foster qualities she herself lacks, but admires in her talented charge, the Cheerleader becomes overly encouraging and overly demanding.

At a time when finding a caregiver who cares enough is a problem for most parents, it may seem churlish to warn against one who cares too much. But often such a caregiver becomes so intent on fostering the toddler's skills, she begins to overlook his need for the hugs, kisses, holding, and other nurturing behaviors that tell a child he is loved unconditionally.

The best antidote to an already developed Cheerleader pattern is to tell the caregiver (as gently as possible) that while you're aware that your child has some remarkable qualities, what he needs most at this point in his development isn't cheerleading, but an understanding, supportive, and uncritical helpmate. A better strategy still is to take steps to prevent the problem from arising. The most effective way to do that is, before making a final hiring decision, to spend a few days observing the new caregiver with the A. Do her expectations seem appropriate to his age and abilities? Is she able to penetrate his Type A aura of competence and see the vulnerable child underneath? Is her praise and encouragement contingent solely on his ability to live up to her expectations? Before giving a final "yes" to the caregiver, its important for a parent to satisfy herself on each of these important issues.

### Do It Yourself

This pattern occurs more frequently among daycare workers than single-child caregivers, and it takes its name from the expectation that the able-looking 3- or 4-year-old Type A is better equipped than his peers to look out for himself in the hubbub of a busy daycare center. This expectation manifests itself in varying ways from one worker to the next. More often than not, in addition to expecting the A to be able to dress himself and find the toys he wants, frequently she also expects him to possess emotional competencies that are equally rare for his age group, such as the ability to amuse himself for prolonged periods of time, to find a place for himself within the group, and to soothe and comfort himself when he's upset.

A particularly graphic example of this last expectation is the response Robert Di Pino, one of my 4-year-old A's, got after an ominous-looking stranger (who was, in fact, an unshaven deliveryman) suddenly intruded on his daycare group's midmorning juice break. Although Robert was as frightened by the intrusion as his peers were, unlike them, he maintained his composure during the incident. Therefore, he was the last child in the group to be taken aside and comforted and the only one the daycare worker didn't encourage to talk about the fears the incident had inspired.

In fairness to Robert's daycare worker and to others who become ensnared in Do It Yourself, a principal culprit in such neglect is often the worker-to-child ratio in many centers. With responsibility for fifteen or twenty toddlers, frequently a daycare worker has no choice but to do what Robert's did after the stranger's intrusion—institute an emotional triage system, which leaves the able-looking A last in line for comfort and support.

In the short run, the effects of this behavior vary from child to child. In Robert's case, for example, it produced a near-phobic reaction to the doorway where the stranger had appeared, as well as regressive behavior and sleep difficulties. But in the long run, its effects are nearly always the same. Because, like the Hurrier parenting style, a last-in-line policy saddles the child with an all-but-unmeetable expectation for emotional competence, it almost always increases his vulnerability to negative Type A behavior.

In cases where the pattern already has manifested itself, the best policy is to point out to the daycare worker that, despite your Type A's in-charge, competent manner, his nurturance needs are no different from other children's, and that neglecting them produces the same unhappy consequences. But, as with Cheerleaders, the most effective antidote to the problem is prevention, which can most effectively be accomplished by selecting a daycare center with a low child-to-worker ratio, if at all possible.

### Control . . . Who's Got the Control?

One of the first things people notice about the Type A child is that he has a strong need to control. This seems to be a by-product of his drive and ambition, and it manifests itself, as such needs usually do, in a desire to feel in charge. Even a 3- or 4-year-old Type A likes to feel he is the undisputed captain of his destiny. Control . . . Who's Got the Control arises when such a youngster is placed under the wing of a caregiver who also has a strong control need. Like Who's the Boss?, it arises not from the sky-high expectations of others, but from a particularly unhappy pairing of personalities.

Deborah Malone, the mother of one of my 5-year-old A's, can attest to just how unhappy this personality combination is. At first, Darlene, the caregiver Deborah hired last year, seemed the answer to a prayer. Darlene was neat, punctual, meticulous, and very orderly. But when this orderliness led her to ban 5-year-old

Tilly's crayons and coloring books from the living room, the result was trouble with a capital "T."

Although Tilly was scrupulous about observing Darlene's ban on art implements, since nothing had been said about toys, Tilly retaliated by turning the living room into a dumping ground for her dolls and their accessories. When a ban was quickly imposed on these items, Tilly was again scrupulous in observing it, but since nothing was said about clothing, the living room was next transformed into a depository for Tilly's dirty underwear and jeans. Two days later, when a very loud ban was imposed on these items, Tilly adopted a new tactic. Reaching for her hat that night, Darlene found Mario, Tilly's pet hamster, sitting in the crown, chewing a piece of lettuce.

Although this kind of guerrilla warfare isn't a factor in negative Type A behaviors, it can be a leading cause of ulcers in adult noncombatants. Which is why, when it erupts, the caregiver should quickly be taken aside and told that the best way to avoid future power struggles with the control-minded A is to give him a little of what he wants. In Tilly's case, an example of this strategy would be to permit her to bring her dolls and art implements into the living room *provided* that she cleaned up afterward. In the case of the 4-year-old A who can't understand why he isn't allowed to play with the kitchen utensils, one could buy him his own plastic or wooden spoons.

### What a Difficult Baby

Even though it's not unique to future A's, I'm including Difficult Baby here because, like other high-strung infants, the reactive (and especially the highly reactive) child's temperament predisposes him toward the kind of troublesome behavior that sets the Difficult Baby pattern in motion. Cranky and irritable, slow to establish regular eating and sleeping patterns and to respond to comforting or soothing, such a youngster—like all high-strung infants—makes a very demanding charge. Caregiver withdrawal, the Difficult Baby pattern's greatest risk, is often a direct result of this demanding behavior.

While continuing to fill the A's nursing needs such as feeding, changing, and bathing, gradually the caregiver begins emotionally distancing herself from her difficult charge; less and less time is spent cooing, cuddling, and hugging him. Some experts believe it's stretching the point to say that the insecure caregiver-child attachment promoted by such withdrawal can be a factor in negative Type A behavior. But my feeling is that, like an insecure parental attachment, an insecure caregiver attachment can—although in a much less dramatic form—contribute to the insecurity that is a principal driving force of excessive Type A achievement striving.

Type A aside, on one point there is general agreement. In its more extreme forms, caregiver withdrawal can deprive an infant of the emotional nurturance and cognitive stimulation needed for healthy growth.

Pretending the child is a dream to care for when it's palpably clear that he isn't often exacerbates the Difficult Baby pattern, since such parental reticence usually drives the caregiver underground. She spends as much time as she can away from the infant, while assuring you she's at his side very minute.

On the other hand, being open and frank about his problems makes her see you as a resource and ally. The caregiver who views a parent this way will be much more likely to discuss with you the problems she has with her tempestuous charge, instead of trying to pretend they don't exist.

### PEERS

A recent study by Drs. Carol Whelan and Barbara Hecker, two University of California psychologists, explains why children also are susceptible to the Type A effect.

Asked to describe their Type A peers, many of the youngsters in the study group characterized them as good students, athletes, and leaders.

Yet, with one exception, the patterns that characterize peer– Type A relations aren't driven by the sky-high expectations these qualities elicit in adults. Experiences like that of Samantha Barnes, the patient I mentioned in chapter 2, are blessedly rare. However, what often is a factor in such behavior patterns are the resentments and jealousies this good athlete and leader inspires in his friends, and in the Type A's desire to escape them.

### King of the Hill

Like Do It for the Team, King of the Hill's plot line is familiar from a dozen movies. Its protagonist is a cocky hero who, after suffering a humiliating come-uppance, is punished for his brash behavior. What makes this pattern so common among Type A's are the very mixed emotions they evoke in friends. While everyone admires the A's leaderliness and in-charge manner, his swaggering "hey, look at me" attitude often secretly intimidates and annoys other children.

Mike Scott, one of my 11-year-old Type A's, had a recent experience that illustrates how quickly a humiliating defeat can bring this secret annoyance to the surface. Mike's setback took the form of violating a universal but unwritten rule among sixth-graders: You never cry in class. In the middle of a dressing-down by the teacher, Mike Scott, the boy with the biggest head in school, suddenly burst into tears.

The next day, all the secret resentments generated by that big head surfaced with a vengeance. Mike found the words *cry baby* scrawled on his locker, and in the school yard at recess, three boys burst into a chorus of boo-hoos as he walked by. What no one did was offer Mike a word of comfort. If they had, they might have discovered the real reason for his tears: a nasty parental fight the morning of the teacher's dressing-down.

Typically, Type A's like Mike who become ensnared in King of the Hill come from homes where outshining others is actively encouraged. For example, when karate was popular among his set, Susan Scott got Mike a private instructor. A few years later, when music and fashion became an interest among his friends, Susan made sure that Mike was the first child in his group to have his hair spiked and to attend a rock concert.

A sharp increase in achievement striving is the chief presenting symptom of King of the Hill. In hopes of accumulating enough new victories to regain his lost eminence, the A begins turning everything into a contest—even a walk to school. But the hypercompetitiveness such striving produces only adds to his already sizable social problems, because it gives friends and peers one other reason to dislike him.

Outside of being supportive, in the short run there isn't much a parent can do to help a child who has become ensnared in

King of the Hill. However, in the long run there is something very important he or she can do. The best antidote to the isolation Mike suffered, as well as to the insensitive swaggering behavior that caused his isolation, is knowing how to be a good friend to others. Many Type A's lack this knowledge, which brings us to the way a parent can help.

Encourage the Type A to form a friendship with one—and only one—other child. The reason for this single-minded focus is educational. In order to develop a network of friends who can provide support in moments of defeat, the A first has to develop the qualities—such as cooperation, sensitivity, sharing, and empathy—that make a child attractive to his peers. The best place to begin mastering them is within a one-on-one relationship with another child.

### Just Like the Other Kids

This is the polar opposite of King of the Hill. Instead of flaunting his competence and leaderliness, the child hides them because he is afraid that if he's pigeonholed as special, he'll become one of those youngsters who is universally admired, but never invited to parties or rock concerts or baseball games.

Fear of encountering yet another set of sky-high expectations contributes to the A's excessive modesty. Not wanting the achievement pressures he faces at home and in school to follow him through the door of the local McDonald's, he spends a lot of time and energy putting himself down.

Since such behavior represents the antithesis of achievement striving, one thing this pattern doesn't do is foster negative Type A behavior. But, as illustrated by the experience of Bonnie Sadler, one of my 16-year-old A's, it can create another, often equally serious problem.

Bonnie did well enough on her National Merit Scholarship test to qualify as a finalist. But when she took the finalist's exam, her score dropped so precipitously that her mother suspected something was wrong. Three intense mother-daughter conversations later, Sandra Sadler discovered that something was indeed wrong. Bonnie had deliberately thrown the exam because she thought her boyfriend would have problems dating a National Merit Scholar.

A thoughtful parent-child conversation is the best way to help a child like Bonnie. Being socially hypersensitive, boys and girls often misinterpret or exaggerate peer reactions. A parent-child conversation offers a forum for correcting such misinterpretations, particularly if the parent emphasizes that everyone experiences such problems at some point in their lives. He or she can mention an experience from his or her own childhood, where a fear of being too successful proved groundless.

**"I Can't Say No"**

This pattern has its starting point in the sky-high goal-setting style of those around the Type A. Because the adults in his life act as if no challenge is beyond him, in time the Type A not only comes to share this belief, but it becomes a matter of honor and self-esteem for him to accept any challenges that come his way. This is a dangerous mindset for any child to have, but for one who inspires as many expectations as the Type A, it is particularly dangerous because it leaves him no recourse but to say "yes" when a peer asks, "Do you think you could jump down the front porch steps on those roller skates?" or, "Can you beat out the guy in the blue Porsche?"

Beyond urging a youngster in the strongest possible terms to say "no" when friends issue such dangerous challenges, one other immediate step a parent can take is to ask the parents of those friends to tell their children to stop daring and taunting the Type A.

The best antidote to the problem, however, is to promote expectations that foster a healthy and appropriate set of limits. This can be done most effectively by following the guidelines on realistic goal-setting outlined in chapter 8.

# 5

# "Whoever Has the Most Toys When He Dies, Wins": The Type A in Society

Not long ago I saw a TV ad for *Fortune* magazine, which, I think, says a great deal about the values we're teaching our children today. Ostensibly, the ad's subjects were three typical *Fortune* readers: a 28-year-old investment banker, a 34-year-old corporate vice president, and a 43-year-old chief executive officer. But the commercial's real stars were their annual incomes, which, in the case of the banker, an off-screen voice told us, was $175,000; in the case of the corporate vice president, $500,000; and in the case of the chief executive officer, a figure that sounded larger than the Gross National Product of Brazil.

Explicitly, of course, this ad is saying, "Buy *Fortune* magazine, and you'll be as successful as these three typical readers." But what makes it such a telling symbol of our current values is that its implicit glamorization of these individual's wealth signals an important shift in the nature of the American success ethic.

While financial prowess always has been an important route to success in our society, over the past decade it has gradually overshadowed medicine, law, literature, social service, and all other forms of achievement, to become the *only* route to success

**74**

(and hence to the self-esteem and admiration success brings). Today, the first thing one is likely to learn in an article about a well-known TV journalist isn't his views on the world, but the size of his salary; and about a well-known author, not what he's trying to say in his work, but the size of his advances.

Competition, another important element in the American success ethic, also has undergone a subtle but significant shift recently; it has slid into a hypercompetitive Type A concern with rank and status. The next thing one is likely to learn about the journalist is where his salary places him among rival anchors; and about the author, where his advances place him among rival authors.

To understand why I believe these recent changes in our success ethic cast a shadow over the future of every Type A boy and girl, consider the results of some recent cross-cultural studies of Japanese and American adults.

It would be hard to imagine a more achievement-oriented or harder-working society than that of present-day Japan. Yet, these studies show that the incidence of negative Type A behavior among Japanese adults is only 18 percent, compared to 50 percent among American adults, and the incidence of heart disease only 4 percent, compared to 18 percent for Americans.

Unquestionably, a number of factors, including diet, account for these findings. But most of us involved in working with Type A's believe that a key factor is the very different way each society defines success. While the Japanese success ethic emphasizes qualities such as harmony, loyalty, and cooperation, which are associated with a very low incidence of negative Type A behavior and Type A–related heart disease, our current ethic increasingly emphasizes qualities such as exclusivity, rank, and hypercompetiveness—which are associated with very high rates of both.

The other social trends I'll discuss in this chapter aren't quite as worrisome as our redefinition of the American success ethic. However, they are just as Type A-ogenic and just as ubiquitous. One trend, the early education boom, has become so widespread that nearly 3 million toddlers and preschoolers are currently enrolled in some sort of early education-enrichment program. A second, emotional adultification has become so ubiquitous that a significant number of American children now are expected to raise themselves.

Anyone who has followed the child-development literature over the past decade knows that experts on the Type A child aren't the only authorities alarmed about the effects of these trends. Drs. Benjamin Spock, T. Berry Brazelton, and David Elkind have issued warnings about the dangers early education and adultification pose for all children. And just about every pediatrician, child psychologist, and educator I know is concerned about our current glorification of wealth.

There are some special reasons why these trends represent additional, unique risks for the Type A boy or girl. And they begin—as does so much in the Type A child's story—with his or her ability to elicit uncommonly high hopes and dreams. If society expects any child to become richer and more powerful than his peers, it is the Type A. And if it is going to expect any child to be mature enough to raise himself and intelligent enough to benefit from early education, it is again the Type A.

These trends also put the Type A at risk for other reasons. One is that they provide a social sanction for some of his most self-defeating and socially problematic behaviors, such as hyper-competitiveness and excessive achievement striving. They also promote the kinds of psychological stress that can exacerbate his anger and hostility, the most cardiac-toxic aspects of the behavior pattern.

## THE REDEFINITION OF THE AMERICAN SUCCESS ETHIC

Anyone who, like me, was a child in the early 1950s will remember that America in those years was still dominated by memories of World War II and the nation's role in it. This role came to be symbolized, in my young mind and in those of millions of other children, by the old black-and-white newsreels of smiling GIs winding their way through newly liberated French towns as the grateful inhabitants showered flowers and kisses on them.

It was a wonderful image for 8-, 9-, and 10-year-olds to have of their country. And those smiling GIs made wonderful heroes. But they also made something else that, in its own way, was even more wonderful. One of the ways a society tells its young which values it deems essential for a successful life is by celebrating the role models who embody those values. And in the early postwar years, the near-universally celebrated everyman citizen-soldier, with his self-sacrifice, valor, decency, and hatred of tyranny, not only made it clear to children of my generation which values our society deemed essential to success, but they defined a vision of success accessible to all.

By the early 1970s, when I began practicing pediatrics, those smiling GIs had been replaced by a new set of role models, but the vision of success they represented hadn't changed, and neither had its accessibility. Not everyone could be a John Kennedy or a Martin Luther King or a Jonas Salk, but you didn't have to be them to achieve the kind of success they represented. All you had to do was fight racism, poverty, injustice, and disease as stoutly as they had.

Now, the wheel has turned yet again, but this time the success model it has thrown up defines success in a very narrow and exclusive way. Today, even a 5-year-old knows that in America, success has come to be defined solely in terms of material well being, as that old adage puts it, "Whoever has the most toys when he dies, wins."

One school, made up mostly of economists, sees the adoption of this Type A standard of success as a necessary and inevitable response to the nation's recent economic decline. Funneling talent to the areas of national life where it is most needed is a success model's principal function, argues this school, and at a time when our standard of living is under assault, it's natural that American society would celebrate a view of success that channeled the ablest of our young into economic activities.

A second school, largely made up of social critics such as Christopher Lasch *(The Culture of Narcissism)* and writers such as Tom Wolfe *(The Me Generation* and *Bonfire of the Vanities),* believes that the adage on that T-shirt reflects America's growing narcissism. According to this school, in a culture where the self is glorified, often at the expense of the community, it is inevitable that the narcissistic pursuit of wealth would come to be seen as a social good.

Whichever theory is correct—and I think both contain elements of truth—one thing is certain: America today has found some ingenious ways to tell even its youngest member, "Here's how your society defines success, and here's what you need to do to achieve it."

One way, for example, is through the accomplishments it chooses to celebrate in the young person's heroes. When a child sees his favorite baseball player lionized, not because he's a twenty-game winner or has a .350 batting average, but because he's signed a $23 million contract, it doesn't take that child very long to conclude that success in his society is measured not by what a person does or how well he does it, but simply by how much he makes.

The ubiquitous lists of "who makes what" that currently fill our magazines and newspapers (recently I saw a list of the ten highest-paid college presidents), also tell a child something important about the present nature of achievement in America. Success isn't defined just by the amount of your wealth, but by where it ranks you among your peers.

As political analyst Kevin Phillips notes in his book *The Politics of Rich and Poor,* not since the Gilded Age of the 1890s have status symbols been so important to Americans. As a child watches the adults around him vie with one another to acquire these symbols, he learns another important lesson about the nature of success in America today: People will consider you a better, worthier person than your neighbor if you drink a more expensive brand of mineral water than he does.

Some figures from Mr. Phillips's book delineate another important feature of our current success model. Its attainment has become immensely harder and immensely more rewarding. While the income of the poorest 40 percent of Americans declined more than 10 percent in the past decade, and the middle class stayed even only by putting another breadwinner into the work force, Mr. Phillips reports that the wealth of the top 1 percent of Americans increased by 74.2 percent.

Mr. Phillips's last figure brings us to the most obvious reason why our new success model poses a special danger to the Type A child: If any boy or girl will be pushed, coaxed, and groomed to fight his way into the charmed 1 percent, it will be the Type A. But the model also poses two other subtle dangers to him. The first is that it removes the social constraints that once put a check on some of the Type A's most aggressive achievement striving and hypercompetitiveness. If the Wall Street financier, who describes his wealth as "just a way of keeping score," is rewarded for his wisdom by being put on the cover of *Time* or

*Newsweek,* how can a parent tell a child like Billy Cronin he shouldn't judge a friend by the size of his house or by the kind of car his parents drive? And if the real estate tycoon who defines the art of the deal as "sticking" your competitors also is glamorized by the media, how can a parent tell a child like Alexi Blondi that trading packs of bubble gum for votes is not the way to win an art contest, but that drawing the best picture is.

The greatest danger our present view of success holds for the Type A is that it presents him with a new and irresistible sky-high goal. If society says that the esteem, admiration, and security you crave can be won by fighting your way into that top 1 percent, millions of Type A boys and girls will set their sights on achieving that goal. But because it is, like many of the other goals in their lives, an impossibly high one, millions will fail. When Stanford University's Dr. Carl Thorenson recently warned *Psychology Today* that we are imperiling the well-being of the Type A child, he had in mind the likely fallout from this high failure rate.

It will include the millions of A's who will spend their adult lives embittered and very angry that that top 1 percent eluded them, and it will also include the millions more whose anger at their failure becomes so great that their risk of heart disease will increase.

Even the A's who do slip into the charmed 1 percent will lose, because they will become so caught up in the pursuit of acquiring still more that, in time, the stresses their striving produces will bring out the most troublesome aspects of their personalities, including the most problematic of all, the risk of a heart attack at 38 or 40.

The rest of us also will pay a price for the Type A child's affinity for our current success model, because there will be a paucity of people to enlighten, lead, inspire, heal, and teach us. Somewhere among today's Type A children are the future Picassos, Hemingways, Einsteins, Martin Luther Kings, Betty Friedans, John Deweys, and Franklin Roosevelts, but these youngsters will never fulfill their potentials unless society begins telling them *now* that writing a great novel, painting a great picture, curing the ill, housing the homeless, healing the sick, and educating the young are just as important measures of success—and maybe even more important—as making more money than everyone else.

## EMOTIONAL ADULTIFICATION

It's twenty minutes before takeoff time. I'm strapped in my seat, about to snap open my briefcase, when I feel a sudden jolt and look over to see a little boy with large dark eyes and a bewildered expression plopping into the seat beside me. His name is Alan, he is 6 years old, and the first thing he does after introducing himself is ask whether he can hold my hand during the takeoff.

"I'm glad you asked," I say. "Takeoffs scare me, too."

As it turned out, Alan and I were still holding hands—and talking—as our plane circled Portland, Oregon, five and a half hours later; by then I'd become so concerned about my seat-mate that I couldn't get his worried little face out of my mind for the next few days.

How had Alan's meeting with the father he hadn't seen in nearly a year turned out? And how had it gone with his father's new girlfriend, Sharon, whom he'd be meeting for the first time? And what would happen to Alan if on the return flight to New York he didn't meet a stranger who'd take the time to hold his hand and talk to him?

Over the next few days also I found myself thinking about the process that had raised these troubling questions for Alan. It's called emotional adultification, and while I discussed one aspect of it in chapter 3, I want to return to it here, not only because, like Dr. David Elkind, author of *The Hurried Child*, I consider it a major factor in negative Type A behavior, but because in the talks I give from time to time to parents' groups, I encounter a good many misconceptions about its sources.

While many mothers and fathers are aware that actively co-opting a child into an adultlike confidant, as Rebecca Little did, often produces stresses no youngster is mature enough to absorb, very few are aware that emotional adultification also has a second, more subtle, equally common source. In this case, the child isn't asked to help shoulder a parental concern, but is, like my seatmate Alan, simply left to his own devices because there isn't a grown-up available to help mediate the large stresses and anxieties all children occasionally encounter.

What makes the Type A so vulnerable to this form of adultification are his manner and his demeanor. If any child looks capable of dealing with adult stresses and worries, it is the Type A. What makes adultification especially problematic for him is that if any child is susceptible to the adult-size stresses the process creates, it is the high-strung Type A.

I realize that what I'm saying may sound incriminating, particularly to working parents. Let me emphasize that the most important elements in the parental buffer boys and girls rely on to reduce large fears and worries isn't shared time, but rather a deep sense of parental involvement and a rich family life.

The results of a recent Australian study of 8-, 9-, and 10-year-old flood victims showed how a rich family life can ease even the most devastating stresses and anxieties. If the experiences of other disaster victims were a reliable guide, the signs of severe emotional trauma these children showed in the weeks immediately following the flood would increase over time. But on follow-up a year later, much to their surprise, investigators found that the children were largely symptom-free. What caused the unexpected change? After considering all the possible causes, the research team concluded that the key one was the parental stress buffer.

Despite their pressing responsibilities, which included rebuilding devastated homes and farms, the parents of these youngsters always found time to listen to their anxieties about what had happened and their fears about what the future held. Given what the children had gone through, this may not sound like much. But, as the investigators noted, a lot more goes on in such parent-child conversations than meets the eye. By showing involvement and concern for a child's emotions, the parent is doing more than offering momentary reassurance. His or her behavior tells the youngster what every boy and girl needs to hear in order to absorb large stresses: "No matter what, you can always count on Mom and Dad to be there when you need them."

The other factor in the buffer—a rich family life—played a more subtle but equally important role in the children's speedy recovery. This is the aspect of the buffer that does require parental time. Mothers and fathers don't realize it, but a lot of what they do in family situations—even if it doesn't directly involve the youngster—helps him absorb stress. And the lessons these Australian parents taught through their role modeling illustrates a major reason why this is so.

The researchers concluded that watching their mothers and fathers cope with their stress at the dinner table, over the barbecue, and in front of the TV had taught the children how to cope with theirs. Similarly, watching their parents reach inside themselves to find the extra strength to go on had taught the children how to find that extra measure of strength in themselves.

Thankfully, very few youngsters ever will have to face the kind of emotional trauma these Australian children did. But merely growing up is so complicated that many aspects of it, such as social anxieties and concerns about one's awakening sexuality, can produce adultlike stresses. Today's culture and media have augmented these traditional stresses with new ones of their own.

Consider, as a case in point, the feelings likely to be evoked in an 8-year-old by the sexually explicit or drug-related lyrics of many of today's songs.

Or consider the feelings likely to be evoked in that 8-year-old by the body count from these recent action films:

| | |
|---|---|
| *Die Hard Two* | 120 deaths |
| *Total Recall* | 42 deaths |
| *Rambo III* | 47 deaths |
| *Batman* | 29 deaths |
| *RoboCop II* | 71 deaths |

Or consider the feeling likely to be evoked in a child of any age by a divorce, by a boy- or girlfriend who demands sex or drug use because everyone else is doing it, by entering an empty house each afternoon, or by news of yet another robbery or mugging in the neighborhood. All of these situations, which are a common part of growing up in America today, produce stresses and anxieties no child can handle without adult help. There are two major reasons why such help isn't as common as

it once was in American homes. The first is the changing structure of the American family, particularly the rise of the two-
career family.

Although work doesn't have to remove the umbrella of parental protection (it didn't for the Australian children), the fact
is that in many families today it does—either because at the end
of the day the parents are too tired or preoccupied to interact
with each other or with their child in a way that helps him
handle stress, or because work removes them from the home for
fifty to sixty hours each week.

A recent article on architecture in *Atlantic Monthly* highlights
a second major reason for the demise of the parental stress
barrier. Talking about recent changes in home construction, a
Marin County builder noted that the principal one has been the
separation of the parents' and children's bedrooms. "Parents
used to want the kids' room right next to theirs," the builder
noted, "but not anymore. Today most ask to have the kids' room
at the other end of the floor because they don't want their
privacy disturbed."

The narcissism this builder was describing often makes a
parent emotionally unavailable to her child. And a frequent
result of this unavailability are outbursts like the one that
marred Candy Michaels' ninth birthday party. As usual, Candy's
parents, Mark and Ariel, had planned the perfect party. They
got the right clown, the right party favors, and the right cake,
but these preparations and the planning of an upcoming trip to
Jamaica so preoccupied them that they didn't notice Candy's
loss of appetite and her lethargy in the week before the party.
These were signs of worry. Candy's best friend's parents had just
announced plans to divorce, and she feared, as children in her
position often do, that Mark and Ariel would be next. If the
Michaelses had noticed Candy's changed behavior, they could
have quieted her fears, but they didn't. So Candy's worry grew
and grew until finally it got so big it spilled out at the birthday
party. Instead of squealing in delight when Mark and Ariel
wheeled out her "big present," a ten-speed bike, Candy burst
into tears.

I thought about the Michaelses recently when I saw *My Left
Foot,* the movie about the life of the Irish artist and writer
Christie Brown. While the elder Browns didn't enjoy the

Michaelses' advantages of education and affluence, they possessed a near genius for creating a rich family life and for being there for a child who had enormous needs. The result was the miracle of Christie Brown, a boy who rose above cerebral palsy, to lead a rewarding, productive, and important life.

In his book *The Hurried Child*, Dr. David Elkind declares behavior like the Michaelses' to be an important source of negative Type A behavior because it leaves a child exposed to the kinds of big anxieties that can overstress a reactive temperament. I agree. But I think the decline of the parental stress buffer may have an even more serious consequence for Type A's.

The reason: Emotional adultification often exposes the Type A boy or girl to a double stress. If any youngster will be expected to be able to handle the big emotions raised by a cross-country flight, or a divorce, or the songs of a rap group like 2 Live Crew, it will be the Type A. This means that, besides having to deal with the stresses these situations produce in themselves, he also has to worry about living up to everyone's expectation that he is stronger and more mature than other children.

I think this double stress may be why my seatmate Alan's visit didn't turn out to be as happy as his father had hoped. At the airport, when I handed Alan over to him, I gave him the phone number of my hotel and told him to call me when he settled on a date for Alan's return. Maybe we could fly back together, I thought.

I never got a call, but about a month after my return to New York, I got a note from the father. He thanked me for my kindness in keeping Alan company during our flight and apologized for not getting back to me. He said that Alan had seemed so stressed and anxious during the visit that he felt it would be too much to ask him to take another long plane ride without a family member. So, he'd decided to take a few days off and bring Alan back to New York himself.

### THE EARLY EDUCATION BOOM

Advocates of early learning don't say why a baby needs to learn how to read or think abstractly, but, judging from the recent *thousandfold* increase in early-learning programs, they don't need to. Many parents have already convinced themselves that reading, swimming, spelling, karate, and similar activities can benefit a 1-, 2-, or 3-year-old.

But can they?

A recent visit to one of the meccas of the early-learning movement left me unconvinced. Outside the classroom, the parents I saw showed an intuitive awareness of the young child's need for a relaxed, playful, uncritical parenting style. But inside, the process of formal instruction in reading and spelling made them forget what they knew about this need. They displayed the directive, critical, intense parental style that baffles and distresses a 1-, 2-, or 3-year-old.

One other thing I noticed during my visit to the early learning center was how many of its young students were nascent Type A's. And while I wasn't surprised—after all, who looks better equipped to struggle with the rigors of math and reading—it did trouble me because of all children, the A is most vulnerable to two chief dangers of early education: a distrust of the parental environment and fear of failure.

Given the number of experts who have warned about its dangers—and they include some of the nation's most eminent pediatricians and child psychologists—the popularity of early learning may seem baffling, but there are reasons why it's hard even for skeptical parents to resist it.

The first is status pressures. Among middle-class parents in particular, karate for 4-year-olds, swimming for 2-year-olds, and reading for 18-month-olds has acquired such social caché that it is difficult, even for the parent who knows better, to check the impulse to keep up with the Joneses educationally.

A conversation I had recently with the mother of a 2½-year-old patient provides a case in point. "I'm not entirely happy about putting Keri [her daughter] into Gymboree," the woman said. "It doesn't offer any exercise she isn't already getting tumbling around the living room floor. But I don't have an alternative. I would rather spend the money than be the only parent I know who doesn't have her child in Gymboree."

More substantially, parental fears about downward mobility also have helped fuel the boom. Not that anyone expects a Gymboree class to put a child first in line for law or medical school, but many parents do think early education has a kind of domino effect. A reading or spelling class now will open the door later to a good nursery school, and that in turn will open the door to a good grammar school, high school, and college, which will open the door to a good job.

Some of the recent discoveries about infants' and toddlers' intellectual competencies have also inadvertently contributed to the boom. I say inadvertently because, while the new research does show the young child to be an able learner, particularly in social and play situations, somehow on the journey from the laboratory to the pages of many popular parenting books, this finding has undergone a strange and guilt-inducing transformation. Instead of picturing the baby as the able, natural learner he is, these books present him as a kind of infant-intellectual who comes into the world with a need to read and write as elemental and urgent as his need to eat and sleep.

Dr. T. Berry Brazelton wasn't talking specifically about the Type A when he said recently, "At what price are we forcing our two-year-olds to recite numbers and our three-year-olds to read?" But he might as well have been because, of all children, the A is most vulnerable to early education's two principal dangers.

Take the first—the distrust of the parental environment it promotes. Like the mothers and fathers at the early learning center, most parents forget what they know about the young child's needs the minute they take out the flashcards and alphabet tables. Instead of being relaxed, accepting, and nurturing, they become directive, critical, demanding, and teacherly. And because this behavior puzzles the infant or toddler, who's programmed to expect something else from his parent, he becomes distrustful and insecure. On some level, he thinks, "I guess I can't trust Mom and Dad to understand my needs. Maybe it's because they don't think I'm important enough to try to understand."

What distinguishes the nascent Type A isn't that other early learners don't think those same thoughts when placed in front of a flashcard, but rather the unique history he brings to his reading of the card. Even though the fault lies in his reactive temperament, he's already suffered one major expectation violation: The failure to meet his nurturance and soothing needs and the residue of insecurity it has left makes him perceive the card differently from other children. Instead of viewing it as an aberrant example, he's likely to view it as still further proof of the environment's disregard for him and his needs, and this perception heightens his insecurity.

Fear of failure—the second major danger produced by early learning—arises from its square-peg-round-hole aspect. By that I mean, since 1-, 2-, and 3-year-olds aren't cognitively equipped for formal learning, when they try it, they often fail. What distinguishes the Type A from other early learners isn't that he fails more than they do—being intelligent, he may fail less—but the special way failure resonates in him. While it produces an "ouch" in all young children (which is why experiences that expose them to it should be avoided), early and frequent exposure to failure in a child who already associates failure with loss of parental love and feelings of unworthiness produces more than an ouch. It produces such pain that, over time, the child frequently may develop an almost phobic reaction to it. A lot of the excessive achievement striving in 8-, 9-, and 10-year-old A's can be explained not in terms of what they want to get, but of what they want to avoid.

## THE DECLINE OF SOCIAL VALUES

On this raw February night, the subway platform at Thirty-fourth Street and Seventh Avenue is crowded to overflowing with people, many of them prosperous, warmly dressed suburbanites who, like myself and my son Matt, have just come from a New York Knicks game and are awaiting a train home. Sprinkled among us, however, is a second quite different crowd. Its members are ill-kempt and poorly dressed, a few even lack the basics of shoes and socks, and all look ravaged and hollowed out by hunger and cold—and by the thought that they won't be going anywhere tonight or tomorrow night or the night after, because they don't have a home beyond this desolate, foul-smelling station.

Matt, who has never before encountered such poverty first-hand, is stunned by the scene at the station. Ever since we entered, he has been unable to take his eyes off a young woman who's trying to make a bed for herself and her child out of what looks like the remains of a large cardboard box. She neatly folds the flaps together, places a soiled rose-colored blanket over the back of the box, then places a pillow on the blanket. After she puts her child on the blanket, Matt turns to me.

He looks stricken. "Dad, why isn't anyone helping these people?"

"They do get help," I say (a bit defensively). "New York City has shelters, and thousands of people contribute food and clothing to them."

Matt, however seems unconvinced. "If that many people care," he says, "why are so many homeless here tonight, and why do they look so hungry and cold?"

I try again. But still Matt seems unconvinced. And, in truth, I can't blame him. Children's ideas about social values such as compassion, altruism, loyalty, and responsibility are in large part shaped by what they see and hear in the larger society around them, and what our children are seeing in our society now is telling them that in late twentieth-century America, social values don't count for much.

This is a dangerous message for a society to send to any child, but it is an especially dangerous one for the Type A child, because altruism, cooperation, and compassion can have an important effect on reducing his risk of heart disease.

Today, however, even the parent who knows this and who, in response, goes out of her way to promote such values in her Type A finds that she is undercut by the larger society at every turn. Take that scene in the subway station. How can I tell 11-year-old Matt, "Compassion is important," when it's self-evident even to a 5-year-old that his society allows tens of thousands of children to sleep in subway stations each night?

Or consider the behavior of the role models society holds up to today's children. How can a parent tell her youngster, "You are also responsible to your community," when these figures, whom society is so palpably and constantly encouraging the youngster to emulate (mostly by bombarding him with stories and pictures of them), don't feel that responsibility.

Pick up just about any issue of *People* magazine and you'll see what I mean. Whereas once the wealthy had themselves photographed in front of newly funded libraries, hospitals, and universities to advertise their commitment to the traditional American belief that with great wealth comes great social responsibility, today's rich have themselves photographed in front of newly acquired Boeing 747s and fifty-room estates to advertise their commitment to the belief that with great wealth comes the responsibility to indulge oneself.

Or take as yet another case in point the behavior of the sports figures so many of our children idolize. How can a parent insist that loyalty is an important virtue when her youngster hears that his favorite pitcher, the one who last week swore undying fidelity to the team, announces this week that he's exercising his free-agent option. Or, what strikes even closer to home, how can a child be expected to put much stock in loyalty when he sees that his parents or his friends' parents put so little stock in it they jump from job to job and spouse to spouse.

I realize that there are many exceptions and extenuating circumstances in the examples I've cited. Some wealthy people still believe that great wealth confers great social responsibility, and many job changes and divorces are justified. Nonetheless, the fact remains that the message currently emanating from every nook and cranny of American society is no longer the biblical injunction, "Do unto others as you would have them do unto you," but the Type A maxim, "Me first, all others last."

According to one group of experts, this change is due to the growing anonymity of American life. They argue that in our increasingly urban nation, where one can go six months without seeing a next-door neighbor, a decline of communal and social values is inevitable.

I agree that this has been a factor in the change. But I think author Andrée Brooks touched on an even more important reason for it in her book *Children of Fast Track Parents*. Like the house builder I quoted earlier, Ms. Brooks thinks much of our current selfishness has its roots in the baby boom generation's narcissism. I don't want to sound like I'm singling them out for special criticism. Their generation has contributed much to the richness and diversity of American life. Nonetheless, I believe Ms. Brooks is right when she says that the excessively child-centered culture of mid-century America, which reared them, fostered a strong streak of narcissism. I also believe that she is right in saying that now that the baby boomers are assuming positions of authority and power, this narcissism has begun to influence the tone and quality of American public and social life.

How does such a narcissistic society heighten a Type A child's risk of heart disease?

The answer to this question has its starting point in a finding from a recent study by researchers at the State University of New York at Buffalo and Washburn University in Kansas. Assessing the risk of heart disease among adult Type A's, the researchers found one unvarying connection: the lower the A's self-esteem, the higher his likelihood of incurring cardiovascular disease.

What links this finding to our increasingly narcissistic society is that it deprives the A of a key source of self-esteem: the love, gratitude, and appreciation you earn when you reach out and help others.

At other times in our history when values such as loyalty, cooperation, altruism, and self-sacrifice carried greater weight, the Type A discovered the connection between helping others and high self-esteem, in a sense despite himself. His first or even second impulse might not have been to reach out to help a friend or neighbor in need, but communal values carried such weight then that he felt he had to—if only for appearances' sake. And frequently he noticed a connection: the more he helped his friends, colleagues, and co-workers, the better he felt about himself.

Now that these values have been replaced by narcissism, however, the opportunity for the Type A child to make these discoveries about the esteem-boosting power of compassion and caring has been lost, and with it an opportunity to escape the cardiac-toxic anger and hostility, which the SUNY-Washburn study shows is the chief by-product of low self-esteem in a Type A.

What makes these traits so cardiac-toxic?

That question is the subject of chapter 6.

# 6

# The Angry Heart

One important element in the Type A's story remains unexamined.

In chapters 1 through 5 I discussed the origins of the A's insecurity and low self-esteem, the ways in which the environment acts on them, and how these interactions produce the five traits that define negative Type A behavior. What remains unexplored is why this particular group of traits—more accurately, two elements in it, anger and hostility—predispose the Type A child to an increased risk of heart disease, not immediately, it's important to emphasize, but at ages 35 to 45.

The reason lies in the A's reactivity and the way anger and hostility, in particular, impact on it. Type A's are high-strung, and this predisposition expresses itself not only behaviorally but physically. An anxious, frustrated, impatient, or angry Type A not only acts more anxious, frustrated, impatient, or angry than a like-minded Type B; these emotions produce sharper physiological reactions in him. And these physiological differences become particularly sharp when the emotions in question are anger and hostility.

To illustrate how this difference raises the Type A's cardiac risk relative to that of a Type B, imagine the following scenario.

Two 15-year-olds (I'm using teenagers because their near-adult physiology and anatomy duplicates the results of studies which have tracked the physiological reactions of hostile Type A's, well-adjusted Type A's and Type B's), hostile Type A Bobby and Type B Billy, are playing Super Mario on a laboratory Nintendo set. Suddenly I appear in the doorway and make both boys very, very angry by ordering them to do the multiplication problems lying on the table next to the Nintendo set. Then, from behind me, a group of technicians suddenly appears and begins monitoring the physiological changes the boys' anger is producing.

In one sense, my technicians won't find any differences between Bobby and Billy. In all human beings, extreme anger and hostility produce three distinct, unvarying physiological responses: blood pressure and heart rate rise, and the body increases production of its two "crisis" hormones, epinephrine and cortisol. Also, in all human beings, two of these three elements—increased blood pressure and increased hormone secretion—are potentially cardiac-toxic.

Increased blood pressure is potentially dangerous because at high levels it so stresses the arteries that tiny hairline cracks and fissures develop in their walls. And the more cracks and fissures in their walls, the more potential lodgment sites for the bad artery-clogging cholesterol LDL, or low-density lipoprotein. Increased hormone secretion can be dangerous because it too leads the body to produce more LDL.

With these dangers in mind, now let's look at the three differences my imaginary technicians have found in hostile Type A Bobby's and Type B Billy's anger responses.

One was in *intensity*. Because of his reactivity (or high-strung physiological system), Bobby's blood pressure and heart rate rose much more dramatically than did Type B Billy's, and so did his body's production of epinephrine and cortisol. Thus, during the outburst, Bobby's cardiovascular system took a much more damaging "hit" from his anger in the sense that his higher arousal level has the potential to produce more cracks and fissures in his arterial walls and more of the bad cholesterol, LDL, to fill them up.

The second difference involved *duration*. Long after Billy's cardiovascular system returned to normal, Bobby's was still aroused, and long after Billy's body had shut down production of epinephrine and cortisol, Bobby's still was manufacturing them at an increased rate. Thus, during the outburst, Bobby's cardiovascular system took not only a more intense but a longer hit from his anger.

Another difference my imaginary technicians found involved testosterone secretion. Increases in this hormone also increase the body's production of LDL, and while Type B Billy's testosterone levels barely budged during the outburst, hostile Type A Bobby's increased dramatically, which means his arteries were potentially exposed to a second source of bad cholesterol.

Now, imagine a second scenario, to illustrate another recent discovery about the Type A heart-disease connection. In an earlier version of the behavior pattern, it was held that all five of its traits produced potentially damaging blood pressure and hormonal increases. But if we had my imaginary technicians monitor Bobby at a moment when his impatience was producing great frustration or his hypercompetitiveness great stress, we'd discover what researchers have recently discovered. While each emotion produced some sizable physiological change, it was Bobby's anger and hostility that caused the greatest damage to his cardiovascular system.

At what point do the hits that the child's cardiovascular system take from his anger and hostility begin to create a predisposition to heart disease?

In a 5- or 10-year-old Type A, once the moment of anger or hostility passes, his blood pressure and hormonal and cholesterol levels become indistinguishable from a Type B's. But a recent Louisiana State University study suggests that by late childhood the A's cardiovascular system has taken so many anger- and hostility-related hits that what were transitory changes begin to become enduring.

The 10- to 17-year-old A's in the LSU study had higher blood pressure and cholesterol readings than did their Type B study mates. Translated into the mechanism of heart disease, what this difference means is that by 12 or 13, often the Type A is at risk of developing so many minute cracks and fissures in his arterial walls, and so much bad cholesterol has accumulated in them, that his heart has to work a little harder than another youngster's to move blood around his body.

This does *not*, however, mean that the 12- or 13-year-old Type A is in imminent danger of a heart attack. The cracks and fissures in his arterial walls still aren't that numerous, and the cholesterol lodging in them still is so loose that his heart doesn't have to work that much harder than another youngster's. Fast forward this child thirty years into the future, however, and the danger of heart attack becomes very real.

The reason: Three more decades of anger and hostility—and often the exposure to other risk factors such as smoking and obesity—will now have produced so many cracks and fissures in the Type A's arterial walls, and the cholesterol buildup in them now will be so high, and so hard, that his heart won't get the oxygen and other nutrients it needs to function properly.

Not uncommonly, the endpoint of this scenario occurs when the A blows up at a colleague or curses a slow-moving truck or a supermarket checkout line. The extra little bit of stress produced by his annoyance requires an extra effort from his heart, but because his overworked heart is incapable of giving it, the A suddenly crumples up on the floor or in his car seat with a deep, searing pain in his chest.

Readers of the landmark bestseller *The Type A Behavior Pattern & Your Heart* by Drs. Friedman & Rosenman know that my version of how a Type A arrives at this terrible moment differs from its version in one key respect. My version has only two villains, anger and hostility; the book's has five. However, this doesn't mean that in mine, the other three Type A traits— impatience, hypercompetitiveness, and excessive achievement striving—wear white hats. People don't become angry or hostile in a vacuum; they require a trigger, and as the experience of my Type A illustrates, in negative Type A's, often the trigger is impatience, hypercompetitiveness, or excessive achievement striving.

The more nuanced view of the Type A–heart disease connection I've presented here is the product of what's known as the second-generation-A research, which began in the early 1970s, and which we will follow over the remainder of the chapter. Since heart disease is largely an adult phenomenon, you'll find that little of this second-generation work directly involves the Type A child; however, its discoveries have important implications for his present and future well-being. If you are a Type A yourself, as the parents of many A's are, you'll find that these discoveries also have important implications for your present and future well-being.

To put the research into context, however, you'll need to know something about the genesis of the behavior pattern.

## THE DISCOVERY OF THE TYPE A IDEA

If Type A behavior can be said to have a specific starting point in time, it was in the observation of a San Francisco upholsterer who, one day in the early 1950s, noticed something odd while passing through the waiting room of two of his clients. All the chairs in the waiting room had the same wear configuration. While the cloth on the chairs' backs looked brand-new, the cloth on their seat fronts had been worn to the frame. If the clients had been lawyers or accountants, they probably wouldn't have thought much about the upholsterer's observation that such a wear configuration suggested sitters so stressed and anxious that they were quite literally always on the edge of their seats.

But the clients happened to be two cardiologists, and at that particular moment, Drs. Meyer Friedman and Ray Rosenman were feeling puzzled and dissatisfied.

The reason: the then current state of the literature on heart disease. By the 1950s it had grown quite voluminous and detailed, but there was a very large hole in it. Only half its reported cases could be explained by the mechanistic theories of cardiovascular disease so popular in the 1950s. What was making the other 50 percent of cardiac patients so ill?

Along with their upholsterer's observation, there were several other reasons why Drs. Rosenman and Friedman believed that the missing link in all the unexplained cases of heart attack might be the victims' emotions.

One was an extensive store of folklore and ancient medical literature. References to the role of emotions in heart disease date as far back as the Bible, which contains several graphic descriptions of cardiaclike death in the face of severe emotional trauma (e.g., the passage on Ananias and his wife Sapphira in the fifth chapter of the Acts of the Apostles). Discussion of the connection between heart disease and emotions also figures prominently in the work of several prominent seventeenth- and eighteenth-century physicians, most notably in that of Sir John Hunter, whose pioneering observations about the link proved, in his case, all too prophetic.

In 1793, noticing that arguments with colleagues brought on severe angina or heart pain, Sir John complained, "My life is in the hands of any rascal who chooses to annoy or tease me." Indeed, so it proved. A few months after making this remark, Sir John dropped dead in the anteroom of a London hospital after a heated argument with fellow physicians.

Closer to our own time, several nineteenth-century physicians described what we would call a "coronary-prone personality." In 1890, for example, Sir William Osler, Distinguished Professor of Medicine at Oxford, described such an individual in almost Type A terms. "He is," said Sir William, "not delicate and neurotic, but robust and vigorous, a keen ambitious man, the indicator of whose engine is always at 'full speed ahead.'"

The psychiatric literature of the 1950s also contained several descriptions of the role emotions play in heart disease. When Drs. Friedman and Rosenman began reading it, they noticed a correlation that turned out to be important. An earlier review of their patients' medical records suggested that several personality factors or traits might create a predisposition to serious heart disease. Now, reading through the psychiatric literature on the disorder, they noticed that many studies also made reference to these same traits. They were (1) an almost obsessive need to achieve high, but poorly defined (in other words, sky-high) goals; (2) a love of competition; (3) a hurriedness or preoccupation with time and a desire to get things done quickly; (4) a free-floating hostility; and (5) anger.

Could these traits and the emotions they represented be the missing link in all the unexplained cases of heart disease?

In the late 1950s, Drs. Rosenman and Friedman tested this hypothesis in a half-dozen studies, but the experiment that conclusively established the role of emotions in heart disease and also put the term *Type A* on the medical map was the Western Collaborative Study, which began in 1961. Over its eight-year course, the initially healthy subjects with Drs. Rosenman's and Friedman's five suspect traits developed such higher rates of heart disease, stroke, and angina that at its conclusion even skeptics conceded that, like smoking and diet,

Type A behavior deserved to be considered an independent risk factor for heart disease.

One interesting highlight of the WCS study was the birth of the terms *Type A* and *Type B,* which were adopted for a very practical reason: to win government funding support. Being neutral-sounding, Drs. Friedman and Rosenman thought the terms would be unlikely to set off alarm bells in the government's grant reviewers, who at that time were notorious for their habit of rejecting funding requests for studies that didn't conform to their mechanistic theories about heart disease.

With the publication of *The Type A Behavior Pattern & Your Heart* a decade later, this exercise in grantsmanship quickly became a cultural phenomenon. By the mid-1970s, meditation on, jokes about, and analysis of the Type A personality were so common in the pages of the nation's newspapers and magazines that they threatened to create a media traffic jam.

### THE RISE OF THE ANGER-HOSTILITY HYPOTHESIS

The more nuanced picture of the Type A–heart disease connection I presented at the beginning of this chapter arose from a paradox that confronted the Type A–research community in the years immediately following the publication of the Western Collaborative Study. No one could duplicate its results.

The anger-hostility hypothesis, which governs our current thinking about the heart disease–Type A connection, arose in response to this problem. Its principal authors were young second-generation researchers who began entering the Type A field in the early 1970s. In their view, there was a simple explanation for the failure of follow-up studies to find a link between Type A behavior and coronary disease. Not all of Drs. Friedman and Rosenman's five traits—hypercompetitiveness, excessive achievement striving, impatience, anger, and hostility—produced the extreme physiological arousal experienced by my imaginary Type A Bobby.

The investigators also had a pretty good idea of which Type A traits wore the black hats. Several studies, including a few on Type A children, indicated that anger-hostility–free A's not only benefited from their competitive and achievement impulses (provided that they remained within reasonable bounds) but had normal cholesterol and blood pressure levels as well. Equally suggestive, independent of Type A, there was a large, well-documented body of medical literature on the baleful effects of anger and hostility. This work linked the traits to disorders such as ulcers, but it raised a tantalizing question. Perhaps, in individuals whose insecurities and high-strung physiologies made them especially prone to anger and hostility, these two traits also created a predisposition to heart disease.

Three studies, two done by Duke University internist Dr. Redford Williams and his colleagues, strongly suggested that this might be so. In the first, the Duke team eliminated anger and hostility from the Type A equation (through a statistical sleight-of-hand known as "multiregression analysis") to see how reliably a Type A consisting solely of competitiveness, achievement striving, and impatience predicted for coronary disease. Results indicated only a slight correlation. An equally striking finding emerged, however, when the Duke team reanalyzed their data, this time eliminating everything but anger and hostility from the behavior pattern. Now, suddenly, Type A was once again a reliable predictor for heart disease.

Results from the Duke team's second study demonstrated the cardiac toxicity of anger and hostility in an even more direct way. Looking at a group of Type A's with varying degrees of coronary blockage, the team found yet another striking correlation. Generally, the greater his blockage, the more likely an A was to score high on anger and hostility. Moreover, this correlation turned out to be particularly pronounced in young Type A's. Men 35 to 40, who scored high on the two traits, had three to four times the coronary blockage of other Type A's.

In his book *The Trusting Heart, The Great News About Type A,* Dr. Williams notes that the ubiquity of this last finding suggests that Type A—or rather its anger and hostility components—considerably exacerbates the heart disease process. While cardiac disease usually doesn't become a serious problem for most individuals until their late forties or early fifties, among Type A's serious coronary disease is not uncommon at 38 or 40.

The third study, which was done by Florida State University investigators, wasn't actually a study but a reanalysis. Examining the data from the Multiphasic Risk Intervention Trials, or MRFIT, one of the studies that had raised doubts about the validity of Type A, the researchers found that if the study's Type A subjects were scored *only* for anger and hostility, a very robust correlation emerged between Type A and heart disease.

## THE PHYSIOLOGY OF ANGER AND HOSTILITY

My explanation of Type A Bobby's physiological response at the beginning of this chapter owes much to another facet of the Duke team's work. They were among the first investigators to show that in *hostile* Type A's, anger and hostility produce more intense and longer-lasting physical changes. This work supplied the one critical piece of evidence missing from other studies on anger and hostility: It showed how the two traits actually fostered the process of arterial blockage. Moreover, the Duke team delineated this process in a series of simple, elegant, often ingenious studies.

One example is the piece of research that established the unusual physiological intensity of the Type A's anger response. It was done by Dr. Theodore Dembroski, a psychologist, who often worked with the Duke team, and it employed two unusual research tools—video games and harassment. While a group of Type A's matched their wits against a bank of Nintendo sets Dr. Dembroski circulated among them, making disparaging remarks about their prowess as video players. Although he knew that his behavior would generate a lot of anger in a roomful of win-minded Type A's (that was the point), Dr. Dembroski was surprised by the intensity of the physiological responses this anger produced.

As he circulated among the group, the needles on the cardiac monitors attached to the Type A's recorded what seemed an earthquake. Everyone's heart rate, blood pressure, and hormonal levels rose, and among the A's who had scored high on free-floating anger and hostility in pretest screening, these levels skyrocketed.

The study that established the unusual duration of the Type A's anger response was conducted by Edward Suarez, a colleague of Dr. Williams at Duke. It also involved a form of minor harassment. A group of Type A's were given a set of anagrams and asked to work out the solutions mentally. If you've ever done anagrams, you know they require concentration, so naturally Dr. Suarez's deliberate disruptions were annoying. And this annoyance showed up on the monitoring devices attached to the Type A's.

As with my two imaginary 15-year-olds, Bobby and Billy, and as with Dr. Dembroski's study group, the hostile A's physiological expressions of anger were much sharper, but in this study a second difference emerged. While the dip in the non-hostile Type A's readings more or less corresponded to Dr. Suarez's reversion to good behavior, it was noticed that the blood pressure and heart rate readings of the hostile Type A's remained elevated for several minutes.

LOWERING THE TYPE A CHILD'S RISK OF HEART DISEASE

Recently, an important modification was made in the anger-hostility theory. It is related to the five independent elements that are commonly considered to make up anger and hostility:

> *Cynicism,* or the belief that other people are basically untrustworthy, deceptive, or selfish
> *Hostile attribution,* or the habit of thinking others wish you ill and may even be out to get you
> *Hostile affect,* or feelings of loathing and anger when dealing with other people
> *Aggressive responding,* or the tendency to act (rather than just feel) angry and aggressive when dealing with others
> *Social avoidance,* or the wish to avoid becoming entangled in human relationships

Originally, most investigators felt that all of these components were cardiac toxic, but recent research shows that only some are. Social avoidance and hostile attribution can and often do lower the quality of life, but they do not increase a Type A's risk of heart disease. Cynicism, hostile affect, and aggressive responding, on the other hand, do increase that risk—principally because they create a free-floating anger that is particularly prone to surface in social situations. Someone will say or do something the hostile Type A doesn't like (and is predisposed to dislike, being cynically mistrustful of others), and he erupts in a furious outburst that raises his blood pressure, hormone, and cholesterol levels.

This finding may seem at odds with a point I made repeatedly throughout the previous six chapters: that the principal source of the Type A child's anger and hostility—and hence, the principal source of his cardiac risk—lies in his low self-esteem and insecurity. However, pick up any developmental text and you'll find that social anger and hostility are really a reflection of this deeper self-anger. Think about your own behavior at times when you've felt bad about yourself, and likely you'll understand the accepted psychological maxim: People who don't like themselves don't like anyone else.

Read further into those developmental texts, though, and you'll find that in a child, the best antidote to such negative feelings is a responsive, understanding environment. The reason: Its understanding and sensitivity promote his self-worth, and the better a youngster feels about himself, the more he will reach out to others. Another widely accepted psychological maxim is that the child who's learned to value himself and others has exhausted the major sources of anger and hostility in the human condition.

How does the parent of a Type A build such an understanding and responsive environment?

Research has now reached the point where we can answer that question with some authority. A case in point is a report I mentioned briefly in chapter 1, an ongoing study of grammar school Type A's conducted by Dr. Karen Matthews of the University of Pittsburgh.

Among her positive Type A subjects—that is, among her Type A's who have a strong rather than an angry sense of self—Dr. Matthews finds four environmental elements characteristic: communication is child- rather than parent-centered; discipline always respects the child's dignity; goals are shaped to who the Type A is, not to the hopes and dreams he elicits; and family values offer the A other sources of esteem besides winning.

The principal reason why Dr. Matthews's subjects are the exception rather than the rule among Type A's today is not parental insensitivity but rather parental knowledge gaps.

How, for example, do you discipline with respect a child whose high-strung nature often produces unruly behavior, or meaningfully converse with a child whose distrust of others makes him wary of intimate communication, or set self-esteem–building goals for a child whose achievement impulse makes him vulnerable to sky-high goals? And given the Type A's win-win mindset, how do you help him develop values that will boost his self-esteem from things other than getting the highest grade or longest hit or having the newest Barbie doll or biggest baseball-card collection?

# PART
# II

◆

# The Making of a
# Type A Positive Child

# INTRODUCTION

In the second half of the book you'll find little about how to manage a Type A child's anger, hostility, impatience, and hyper-competitiveness; and if you are familiar with adult Type A therapies, where such management techniques are widely employed, you may find their absence surprising. So, by way of introduction to this section, let me briefly say a word about why the strategies in chapters 7 through 11 take a different approach to the problem of negative Type A behavior.

The principal reason lies in the child's greater malleability. At age 30 or 40, the root cause of negative Type A behavior—a weak, insecure "I,"—is largely fixed and unalterable. But at age 5, 10, or 15, it is not—it can change and grow as much as the child himself can. So the strategies and techniques I've devised largely eschew the symptom management and control that are the mainstays of adult Type A therapy, in favor of the more global aim of promoting self-esteem.

High self-esteem is the key agent in transforming the boy's or girl's developing "I" into a strong, secure one. In the case of the Type A child, the effects of this transformation are unvarying. The better the A feels about himself, the better able he is to enjoy the beneficial parts of his personality and the less vulnerable he is to its negative aspects.

One word of caution, however. It will take six to eight weeks to master the strategies and techniques that follow, and an additional several months before the Type A positive environment they create begins to produce noticeable changes in your child.

Be patient with him and with yourself.

# 7

# A Few Words About
# Some Old Habits and
# How to Eliminate Them

The man in the videotape is trying hard to do something that sounds simple. His name is Tom Falcone, and what he's trying to do is appropriately praise his 10-year-old, Maria, for correctly solving nine of the twelve long-division problems in the workbook she's showing him. What makes this simple task difficult for Tom isn't indecision about what to say. During his visits to my office, Tom's learned enough to know how to praise Maria for her triumph. What he hasn't learned is how to conquer his old desire for perfection. And therein lies the source of his difficulty. Tom is disappointed; Maria didn't get all the problems right, and hard as he tries to hide it, Tom's disappointment undermines his ability to be as encouraging and supportive as he wants to be. Saying, "Very good, Maria, excellent," his voice is dutiful, correct, and just tight enough to suggest how unhappy he really feels.

Tom's problem isn't unique. Often, when a parent first begins using the strategies that make up the second half of this book, he finds himself undermined by his old impulse to demand perfection or to overencourage, overcriticize, overcompare, or overpraise. Just as often, the undermining takes the form of a tendency to send double messages to the child.

**107**

Exhibit A of the double-message phenomenon is Tom's behavior on the video. While his words are appropriately praising, his behavior and tone of voice send a much more critical, disapproving message.

Exhibit B is what I call the flip-flop. A parent thoughtfully praises her youngster for doing his best on a test; then, suddenly seized by the old impulse to compare, she says, "By the way, how did your friend Adam do?"

Exhibit C is the "yes, but" syndrome. A goal is first lauded as appropriate; then, gripped by an impulse to set a sky-high goal, the parent adds, "But I wonder if . . ."

Exhibit A of the child's ability to read these double messages is Maria Falcone, who, on the videotape, responds to her father's praise by asking anxiously, "What's the matter, Daddy, didn't I do well?"

Looking at his daughter's upset face on the video monitor in my office, Tom shakes his head and sighs, "I haven't changed a bit."

In fact, Tom has changed enormously. He's a much more sensitive, caring parent than he was when he walked into my office eight weeks ago. But his old impulses remain a problem for him, as they are likely to remain a problem for you and other readers as you begin to use the goal-setting discipline, communication, and value-promoting strategies that follow.

One thing you should try not to do is feel guilty about these impulses. The desire to encourage, compare, and criticize are normal and natural to all parents. And if, in the case of the Type A's parent, the impulses sometimes become overly enthusiastic, usually it's because the Type A has trained Mom and Dad to respond to him that way.

A more constructive approach to the problem of parental double messages and the impulses behind them are the exercises in this chapter. If the strategies in part 2 of this book can be said to have a single goal, it's to boost the Type A's self-esteem so that he can be all that he's capable of being. And if the ten exercises in this chapter can be said to have a single aim, it's to help you conquer the old habits, which can undermine your ability to use strategies in the way in which they are intended.

Don't expect miracles. The exercises won't magically banish deeply rooted feelings and impulses on first use. However, if you employ them each time you feel the desire to overcriticize or overencourage or set a sky-high goal, I think you'll find what the parents of many of my Type A's have found; that in time the exercises make it easier for you to respond to your Type A child in a single, encouraging, approving voice.

Here's what you can tell yourself:

*When you feel the impulse to criticize:* Put yourself in your child's shoes. Nothing gives a parent a better perspective on his behavior or makes it easier for him to check than a few minutes spent contemplating himself from his 5-, 10-, or 15-year-old's vantage point. This is particularly true in the case of criticism, because once in his child's shoes, a parent finds himself looking up at an all-powerful, all-knowing authority figure, whose powers of approval and disapproval are so great that his faintest smile or rumble of discontent can produce a joy or ache in the child that lasts for weeks. This parental deity is, of course, largely a figment of the vulnerable youngster's imagination, but having spent a few moments contemplating him from a pedestal-eye view, a parent finds that he tends to choose his words more carefully when he offers observation about a report card, test score, or an item of clothing.

As part of perspective taking, you might also think back to a moment when your mother or father criticized you in a particularly harsh fashion. We all have such memories, and evoking them will make the pain that critical words can cause a child vivid and immediate, in a way almost nothing else can.

Just ask Judy Dencer, the mother of one of my 13-year-old A's.

Judy finds that all she has to do to check her impulse to criticize her daughter, Brenda, is think back to her twelfth birthday and how hurt and humiliated she felt when her father came out on the front porch, where she was waiting for her party guests. "Judy," he said, "that new blue dress you're wearing makes you look a little fat; why don't you change into something else before your friends arrive?"

*When you feel the impulse to compare:* The most immediate and direct method is, again, to take perspective. You know what you mean when you ask how friend Billy or Betty did on a test. You're simply trying to show a healthy and appropriate interest in the academic performance of your child's friends. The benefit of taking perspective in this case is that it helps you understand the very different meaning your child attaches to this interest. What makes this understanding a powerful antidote to the comparison impulse is that no parent wants her child to feel she is continually ranking him, and she especially doesn't want him to feel her love and approval will be withheld if he doesn't rank number one.

A second way to check the comparative impulse is to correct the misapprehension underlying it, which is that comparisons are good preparation for the tough, competitive world that lies ahead. These days, especially, such preparation is an important priority for many parents. They know that in our increasingly competitive society evaluation and comparison are the norm, and they see comparisons as a way of providing a taste of the future. If a child is nudged now about Betty and Bob's performance, so the reasoning goes, he'll be better able to stand up to the nudging he'll get later when he's one of three candidates being evaluated for vice president of marketing.

Should you ever find yourself thinking along these lines, there are a couple of things of which you might remind yourself. One is that it's the world's job to teach a child about competition; the home's job to teach him about the power of unconditional love and acceptance. You might also remind yourself that the better the home teaches this lesson, the more likely the child will be to develop the inner strength and self-confidence that are the chief characteristics of a tough, resilient competitor.

For parents who have a special difficulty with comparisons, I also recommend spending some time examining the origins of this impulse. Is it rooted in a need to have a child who is always head of his class? If so, does this need outweigh your child's need for a supportive, loving, accepting environment?

Sheila Klein concluded, "no, it didn't" after one too many parental comparisons to best friend Regan led her 14-year-old daughter, Toni, to snap, "Maybe you ought to be Regan's mother, you obviously like her better than me."

*When you feel the impulse to overencourage:* Try the technique called projection. Before giving way to the desire to push your child into a situation or to impose a goal that might put him over his head emotionally or intellectually, stop for a moment and consider the demands the situation or goal will place on him and his ability to meet them. Parents who take the time to project this way often find themselves making some surprising decisions, as Jonathan Silberman, the father of one of my 8-year-old A's, discovered recently.

Jonathan was thrilled when son Aaron's Little League tryout proved such a dazzling success that the evaluating coaches offered to bump Aaron up to the intermediate division. Within the Silberman household, however, his offer wasn't universally smiled upon. Becky Silberman, for one, had some reservations about letting her 8-year-old son play in a division for 10- and 11-year olds, and in truth, Aaron himself was less than enthusiastic about the offer. Great as his dreams of sandlot glory were, they did not include defending first base against boys who would be three to four inches taller and fifteen to twenty pounds heavier than he. Jonathan, however, was adamant about accepting. And his adamance made him such an eloquent proponent of saying "yes" that in time Aaron began to waiver in his resolve to say "no."

Listening to his father, Aaron started to believe that perhaps he was passing up a chance of a lifetime.

At about this time I entered the picture. Becky Silberman, who was the agent of my intervention, insisted that Jonathan talk to me before a final decision was made on the coach's offer.

During our conversation, I outlined the two principal risks Aaron faced if the family accepted the offer. The first was physical. Aaron's fears of what might happen to him in collisions with bigger, stronger boys were not unjustified. The other risk was to Aaron's self-esteem. Being bumped up a division also bumped up his chances of failing—and failing in front of older boys whose respect he'd crave.

Jonathan remained unmoved, however. "Twenty or thirty years from now," he said, "I don't want Aaron wishing what I sometimes wish, that my dad had pushed me a little harder."

I told Jonathan that I understood his concern and suggested he do one last thing before he accepted the offer. "Go home tonight and spend some time projecting what life will be like for Aaron in the intermediate division," I said. "Put yourself in his place and try to imagine how he will feel the first time an older boy criticizes him for striking out, or the first time he has to defend first base against a hundred-pound eleven-year-old. If you're comfortable with what you see—and by that I mean if you think that Aaron has the emotional and physical maturity to handle the situations he'll find himself in—you and he have my blessing. Accept."

One of the things I've learned about parents is that if you frame a problem correctly for them and give them the right tools to solve it, they will almost always arrive at the right answer on their own. And so it was with Jonathan.

The next morning he told Aaron, "You know, I've been thinking it over. Maybe this offer isn't such a good idea after all. Why don't we let it pass. Plenty of other opportunities will come along."

*When you feel the impulse to overpraise:* Remind yourself that while praise is a normal, natural, and happy parental instinct, too many "terrifics" and "wonderfuls" leave a child feeling that a still more terrific, wonderful performance will be expected of him the next time (which is to say, they leave him feeling that he's just been presented with a sky-high goal).

Or, remind yourself that if you overpraise your child now, later he may, like many adult A's, grow wary, even distrustful of praise.

The research shows that A's, unlike other men and women, often react negatively to commendations and expressions of admiration. Sometimes they brush them aside; at other times, they dismiss them with a shrug. But at all times they react to praise as if they have just been handed something they don't like or entirely trust. Given their early experiences with it, it isn't hard to understand why they react in this manner.

An example of the unhappy personal consequences this distrust can have is provided by a surgeon friend of mine, whom I'll call Bernie Taffel. Bernie is a brilliant doctor, and at the hospital where we both practice he is also the resident curmudgeon. Say something nice to Bernie and he'll growl "hurrumph" and wave his hand in front of him as if he were trying to swat aside your praise the way he would an annoying fly.

Colleagues attribute this habit to Bernie's innate personality. But I suspect it has another source. Sour and argumentative, Bernie is not a happy man. I think that in some measure he isn't because, early on, his distrust of praise made him decide to deprive himself of what is one of life's most pleasurable and satisfying experiences.

*When you feel the impulse to get angry:* There are many forms of parental anger, but this exercise is designed to deal only with the kind that erupts when parental achievement expectations are violated. Not surprisingly, this is the most corrosive variety. One way to put a cap on it, and the impulse behind it, is to remind yourself of the reasons why it is so corrosive: it tends to reinforce the child's view of winning as the only way of earning parental love and esteem, and, as his prime role model, your anger validates your youngster's impulse to get angry at himself when he fails.

Strong emotions such as anger are at times impervious to reason, so on occasion something stronger than a reminder may be required. One simple check is physical removal. If you feel yourself in danger of losing control, tell your child that you have an errand to run or a chore to do and will get back to him and the conversation later. Switching to a less emotionally charged subject, like the family's plans for this weekend, is another way of putting a cap on your anger. Just be sure that if you use this strategy, you tell your child you want to change the subject; otherwise he may be confused by your abrupt switch from one topic to another.

Locating your "hot spots" will give you a third line of defense against your anger. You can do this by mentally reviewing the whats, whens, and wheres of your life with your child, and asking yourself, "Which situations most often set me off?" Some will suggest themselves immediately. Others may not. The mother of one of my patients used to wonder why her daughter avoided her on Sunday nights, until her husband pointed out that Sunday nights was when she and the daughter reviewed the weekend's homework assignment.

"And?" said the woman.

"You always raise your voice," her husband replied.

Besides a raised voice, out-of-character language (being unusually sharp with the child) and behavior (being unusually aggressive and forceful with him) are other common indications that a situation is tapping in to a parent's achievement expectations in a potentially explosive way.

One way to deal with hot spots is to do what this mother did, after deciding that a few incorrect spellings were a lot less harmful to her daughter's self-esteem than were her explosions.

She had her husband take over the homework chores. If changing the situation isn't an option, as, for instance, it isn't at report-card time, there are other ways to deal with hot spots.

One is by mentally preparing yourself beforehand. If you know a situation is always volatile for you, before stepping into it, map out a plan of action, including what you'll do if the worst happens. Knowing what you're going to say if you see a D on your child's report card makes it less likely that you'll say something you may later regret.

Another way to control hot-spot anger is to use the Relaxation Response described in chapter 12. While it's designed primarily to assuage anxiety, its combination of breathing exercises and visual imagery can also be an effective check on almost out-of-control parental temper.

*When you feel the impulse to set a sky-high goal:* Consider what you've learned in the first six chapters of this book. Before setting your next sky-high goal, stop and ask yourself, "Knowing what I know now, can I honestly say this goal is likely to enhance my child's self-esteem, his self-confidence or his feeling that I'm in tune with his needs?"

Another, more general antidote to the impulse is to ask yourself, "How well do my sky-high goals square with my desire to have a happy child?" Most parents don't think of these two goals as mutually exclusive, nor do they have to be; youngsters need and welcome appropriate parental goals. But in homes where sky-high goals rule, usually by age 6 or 7, the two aims have become contradictory, which leaves the parent facing a stark choice. She can step back and let her child do what he needs to do to feel happy—pursue his own goals at his own pace. Or she can continue, and hope that her child avoids the unhappiness almost all children feel when made to pursue someone else's goals at someone else's pace.

Most parents find either of these mental exercises powerful enough to counteract sky-high goal-setting. But if you need a little extra help with this impulse, there are two other exercises you can use.

One is to think about the nature of your Type A child. Given all you know about his drive, energy, and competitive zest, do you think it likely he will choose *un*challenging goals for himself?

The other exercise also involves a question: How do you want to be remembered by your 30- or 40-year-old son or daughter? Do you want to be recalled as the wise, supportive figure whose help and advice allowed the child to be all that he or she wanted to be? Or do you want to be remembered the way a colleague whom I'll call Bill Stanton remembers his father? Bill is a department chairman at the medical school where I teach. Over the years he's become everything his physician father dreamed he'd be. Bill has made a score of important contributions to the field of medical education, he has an international reputation, and his private practice reads like a *Who's Who* of the New York social, political, and literary establishments. But there is a part of him that still longs to be the English professor that he dreamed of being at age 15. And there is also a part of him that still hasn't overcome his bitterness when, at 20, he was forced to pursue someone else's dream for him.

*When you feel the impulse to overcommit your child to classes and activities:* Remind yourself of what I pointed out in chapter 5. Children don't have the emotional—and sometimes intellectual—capacity to handle a full schedule of after-school activities in addition to their normal school responsibilities. Or, remind yourself of a hazard that is equally significant: Over-scheduling can deprive a child of the opportunity to learn how to be comfortably alone with himself. Like most parents, you probably don't think of being alone as a skill, but in fact it is a very important one. You can't read, write, study, engage in any form of play unless you know how to be alone comfortably. There is general agreement that a child learns how to do this best when he's given time to curl up in his room alone with a book or his baseball-card collection, or to waste a Saturday morning hunting grasshoppers in the backyard.

A third line of defense against the impulse to overcommit requires that you consider attaching yourself to a kind of unofficial support group. These days, especially, it's easy for a parent to believe that if her child isn't enrolled in at least four after-school classes a week, she's putting his future in peril. The best antidote to this notion and the unfair guilt it provokes is a like-minded parent who can remind you of what your better self already knows. You're not depriving your youngster, you're just being a good parent to him.

*When you feel the impulse to give way to one of your child's Type A impulses:* You've been in this situation hundreds of times. Your youngster wants something for no better reason than that it satisfies his Type A itch to be out in front of the pack. You know if you say, "No, I think that's unwise or harmful," he'll hit you with a dozen arguments. At these times, remind yourself that even if you let him have the new toy, hairstyle, or pierced ear he wants, you still won't be giving him what he really wants, which is a reason to feel good about himself. This is the desire that drives the insecure A's endless requests for this and that. Keeping this in mind not only makes it easier for you to say "no," but it makes it easier for you to give your child the one thing that will assuage his insecurity—unconditional, all-accepting love.

Of course, on occasion, even very secure, self-confident Type As will want things that are unwise. Being the kind of children they are, their desire for these things will be backed by a will of steel and enough energy to fuel an aircraft carrier. Therein lies the reason why this exercise has a second step. It's called ventilation, and it's designed to help you stick to your "no's" by preventing you from falling into a trap that resisting parents often fall into—rebutting a child's argument point by point. Ventilation transforms you from a debating opponent into a sympathetic listener. You ask your A to tell you about his disappointment. Emotionally, this strategy is akin to releasing air from a balloon. The more the child talks about his disappointment, the less he feels it, and the less disappointed he feels, the less likely he is to continue nudging you about the thing that produced his disappointment.

"Less likely," of course, does not mean "never." On occasion, nothing will dissuade the Type A. He'll want what he wants, period. Provided what he wants isn't egregiously unwise or dangerous, you won't be putting his future at risk if, just this once, you give in and say "yes."

*When you feel the impulse to yell at your child for being so impatient:* You've been in this situation dozens of times. It's a late Saturday morning, and you and your child are preparing to depart for an early lunch at McDonald's, but before you go, you want to finish picking up the house. When he says, "C'mon, hurry up, Mom," remind yourself that you are his role model; a lot of his behavior is shaped by the way he sees you behave, and, as we shall see in chapter 11, a parent who is unable to control her impatience makes a poor role model for a child who is try to learn to control his. At such times, it also helps to remind yourself that your child's impatience isn't a deliberate provocation. His troubles with waiting are an expression of his reactivity, not an attempt to drive you crazy.

However, the best defense against this impulse, is to diffuse the child's impatience before it begins to drive you up a wall. Giving him a chore that will keep him occupied until you finish yours is one way to do that. Knowing exactly when his parent will be ready also makes it easier for the child to control his impatience. Just be forewarned that if you give your youngster a specific time and then fail to finish when you said you would, his impatience is likely to increase exponentially.

*When you feel the impulse to conquer all the impulses you've read about in this chapter simultaneously:* Resist it by reminding yourself of something psychologists have long known—that the best way to alter deep-seated beliefs and attitudes is to chip away at them gradually, step by step and day by day. This is the approach I recommend to the parents of my patients. I urge them to focus first on their two weakest Type A–promoting impulses. If, for example, they find it relatively easy *not* to criticize their child when he does something wrong—or right— and not to overencourage him, I tell them to start by working on these, and when they have conquered them, to move on to two impulses they find harder to resist.

A word of warning: Don't expect immediate success. You're attacking beliefs and attitudes that are a deeply rooted part of your personality. Changing them will take time and effort. However, you'll find that as change begins to occur, you'll be able to use the strategies in the following chapters more effectively.

# 8

# Setting Goals for a Type A

Mention the words *goal* and *Type A* in the same sentence, and most people immediately think of academics. And the Type A child does set high academic goals for himself. But, like other boys and girls, the A's hopes and dreams extend beyond the classroom. There are dozens of other things he wants—from himself, from his friends, from his parents, and from life. And so, like other children, the A's goals also often include getting a certain number of hits per baseball game, or a part-time job, or extra driving privileges, or a later curfew, or being the first 8-year-old in his circle to have roller blades.

Also like other children, goals are a key source of self-esteem to a Type A. Nothing makes him feel better about himself than attaining a challenging goal, particularly, if the goal is one he's set himself and implemented on his own.

What distinguishes the Type A from his peers, however, is that his goals rarely provide the self-esteem, pride, and satisfaction a goal should provide a child. Sometimes this is because the goals are unrealistically high. Instead of resolving to get one hit per game, as another child might, the ambitious A resolves to get three. At other times, it's because neither the goals nor the success he attains in achieving them feel like they really belong to him.

**118**

The reasons why goal setting and implementation take the shape they do in the Type A home is linked to another of the A's unusual characteristics: the Type A effect and the influence it has on his parents. Seeing how ambitious their child is, parents not only support and encourage the high goals the A sets for himself, but they begin setting their own high goals for him. And seeing how important success is to the A, they also play an active role in helping him implement goals. Finally, knowing how crushing defeat can be to a Type A, if he fails to meet a goal, they respond by offering immediate praise and reassurance.

REMD, or Reasonable Expectations Mutually Derived, the strategy I'll discuss in this chapter, takes a different approach to the issue of goals.

• REMD recognizes that when a Type A child or his parent sets goals individually, as they often do, each is much more susceptible to sky-high goal-setting. It also recognizes that when a parent has an overly powerful voice in shaping a goal, as also sometimes happens in Type A homes, the child feels as if the goal is imposed upon him. REMD emphasizes goal setting through a process of mutual negotiation.

• REMD recognizes that when a child gets parental help in achieving a goal, often he feels the success belongs to Mom and Dad, not to him. It gives the Type A almost unlimited freedom to implement his goals, even to the point of failure.

• REMD recognizes that, in moments of defeat, the last thing a child wants is to be praised or even reassured for failing. So, it gives him what he does want: an opportunity to talk about his disappointment, frustration, and pain.

• Finally, REMD recognizes that the parent of the Type A wants to give her child goals that nurture his self-esteem, and it gives a parent the tools she needs to create such goals.

## STAGE ONE: FINDING THE RIGHT GOAL

The key technique in this stage is goal negotiation. Parent and child sit down together, put a proposed goal—whether parent's or child's—on the table, invite the other party to examine it and suggest refinements, then bargain until the goal assumes a shape that satisfies both negotiators.

I know that some parents may have reservations about giving

a child—especially a 5-, 6- or 7-year-old—such a large voice in goal setting. But a large voice is not an equal voice. As senior negotiator, the parent retains the final veto right, as well as the ultimate responsibility for ensuring that the negotiated goal makes the Type A stretch himself a bit, but not so far that he is in danger of hurting himself physically or emotionally.

As junior negotiator, what the child gets from this process is a chance to discover how seriously Mom and Dad take his thoughts and views, an opportunity to put his personal stamp on all goals, whatever their source, and a lesson in realistic goal setting that he'll be able to use when he begins setting his own goals.

What both child and parent get from negotiation is protection from the sky-high goal-setting that arises when there is no one sitting across the table from you to say, "Gee, I don't think that plan sounds very realistic."

Following are the five steps of goal negotiation:

Step A: *Begin by setting a time for negotiation.* This may sound officious—particularly if your co-negotiator is 6 or 7—but announcing that Tuesday evening or Saturday morning has been set aside for a goal negotiation helps to get everyone's thoughts focused on the subject of the meeting. It also shows the Type A how seriously Mom or Dad takes that subject.

Step B: *Discuss the proposed goal from each party's perspective.* If the proposed goal is the Type A's, begin the negotiation by asking him what he hopes to accomplish by it.

Does he see it simply as a way of attaining financial or academic success, or is he—as children often do—using the goal to satisfy some deep-seated, unconscious needs? For example, is the child whose goal is organizing a paper route really just after pocket money, as he says, or is he using the route to satisfy an impulse to feel responsible and entrepreneurial?

As you listen to your Type A explain his goal from his perspective, take careful note of these hidden needs. A knowledge of them will be important later, if it turns out that his original goal has to be vetoed as unrealistic.

As a co-negotiator, another of your responsibilities is to help your child think about his goals in a realistic fashion. For example, in the case of the paper route, you would point out to him that it means having to get up every morning at 5:30, including weekends and snowy or rainy mornings.

You should also suggest refinements that you think can make the goal more workable. Again, in the case of the paper route, this might involve recommending that he take on a partner so that he doesn't have to get up at 5:30 every morning, or suggesting he organize an afternoon route so that he never has to get up at 5:30.

If the proposed goal is yours, the process works in reverse. You begin by explaining why you think it's a good goal, then invite your child to comment. A 7-, 8-, or 9-year-old won't be able to identify your hidden needs (and, as we shall see in a moment, sometimes parental goals have them). But very often he will think of things you have overlooked in setting the goal.

A discussion John Packwood had recently with his son Jeffrey offers a case in point. John wanted Jeff to raise his math average from a C to a B-plus, and given Jeff's consistent B-plus averages in history and English, this seemed an eminently reasonable parental goal. But when John mentioned it to Jeff, Jeff pointed out something that his father had forgotten but knew to be true. Jeff had to work very hard to maintain those B-plus averages, and, unlike math, which came hard to him, English and history were his easiest subjects.

If the child has, as Jeff had in this case, objections to the parental goal, he should be asked for suggestions. How would he change the goal to make it more realistic?

Step C: *Review the refinements and suggestions each party has made to the original goal and find a compromise.* By the time you arrive at this step, several possible versions of the goal should be on the table. Sift through them with your child and assemble a final goal that satisfies both of you.

One real-life example of how the review process works is the way John and Jeff Packwood arrived at their final goal. Over the course of their discussion, two versions of John's original proposal emerged. Jeffrey would maintain his current B-plus average in English and history, and raise his math average from a C to a C-plus. Or, he would keep his English and history grades where they were, and lift his math to a B-minus.

After considering each alternative carefully, the Packwoods

concluded that the one which best suited Jeff's abilities and interests was option two, the B-minus solution.

Deborah and Timothy Danton's deliberations about Deborah's car privileges offer another example of how the review process works. Deborah's original goal was to have unlimited driving privileges. By the time the Dantons arrived at the review process, two variations were under consideration: Deborah could have access to the family car four afternoons a week, between 4:00 and 6:00; or two afternoons, plus one weekend night until 11:00.

Was less more in this case? With her father's help, Deborah concluded that it was. While it would be nice to have a car four afternoons a week, it would be even nicer to drive herself and her friends to a movie or a party on a Saturday night.

When deliberations end in agreement, as the Packwoods' and the Dantons' did, the negotiation should proceed to Step E. When it doesn't they should move on to the next step.

Step D: *Find a suitable alternative goal if the original is judged unrealistic or undesirable.* This is where a knowledge of the child's hidden needs is important. Children in general, and Type A's particular, are never happy when a goal is rejected as unsuitable. But a lot of the disappointment and upset a parental veto produces can be assuaged if the youngster gives an alternative goal that incorporates some of the hidden needs behind the rejected goal.

Take Alan Casey. Admittedly, feeding the family dog doesn't have quite the glamour of Alan's original goal, which was to organize a paper route. Alan's father wisely vetoed this as constituting a sky-high goal for a 7-year-old. But Alan has adjusted quite nicely to his substitute goal because, like his original, it allows him to make a little pocket money. More important, it satisfies Alan's need to feel responsible.

Denise Aberjanassi also wasn't happy when her original goal—an 11 o'clock weekend curfew—was vetoed as inappropriate for a 13-year-old. But, like Alan, she's adjusted quite nicely to her substitute goal, making enough money to pay for a phone of her own, because it also satisfies her craving to feel a little more grown-up.

Timothy Craven's case needs a little explaining, because on

the face of it, Tim's original goal sounds reasonable. He wanted to run for class president. However, parental concern made his father, Frank, veto the goal. Frank knew enough about Tim's social problems to know that he would lose badly, and he knew that with his fragile ego, Tim would be extremely upset by a defeat.

Tim's alternative goal, which Frank fashioned with the aid of Tim's teacher, was to help organize the class's field trip to the Bronx Zoo. Like Alan's and Denise's substitute goals, this proved a success, because it gave Tim an opportunity to feel like a leader.

What if the parent's goal is rejected?

Very rarely will a child say, "I'm not going to do that, Mom," or, "That's too hard, Dad," if he knows Mom and Dad are really serious about a goal. But a youngster who is unhappy about a parental goal will find plenty of other ways to signal his unhappiness. He'll offer a thousand and one objections to it, or he'll stall by saying, "Maybe we shouldn't make a decision tonight," or he'll start to make excuses.

If this happens to you, the first thing you should do is examine your goal in the light of the child's past achievements, age, and developmental stage. Are you asking your Type A to do something children his age normally can't do? Is your goal out of line with the abilities he's displayed?

If you find yourself answering yes to these questions, take a look at your hidden needs. Is your goal perhaps a reflection of your own need for success or for perfection? Are you using the goal to make a point to yourself? This was true for Jonathan Silberman, the father I mentioned in chapter 7. More than anything else, what made Jonathan enthusiastic about pushing his son into an older Little League division was his desire not to behave like his father.

Knowing about parental hidden needs won't magically make them go away. But it will be easier to avoid them if the child's resistance makes it necessary for you to offer him an alternative goal.

Step E: *Once a goal is agreed upon, make sure everyone understands that it is a finite goal.* Because imaginations fly high in Type A homes, goals—even good goals—have a way of taking on a life of their own. What began as an agreement to organize a small paper route can suddenly escalate into a plan to organize an IBM of paper routes. Or, what began as an agreement to raise a social-studies grade to an A-minus can escalate into a plan to maintain an A-minus in all subjects.

The purpose of this final step is to prevent such escalation. You can do this through an exchange of verbal assurances. At the conclusion of the negotiation, the parent should explain what he or she understands the goal to be, and then ask the child what he understands it to be. Another way to implement this step is by putting the agreed-upon goal in writing. Not every family needs to do this, but if there is a history of broken agreements, writing down the goal ensures that there will be something concrete to consult later, if one of the negotiators succumbs to a temptation to raise the goal.

One last point: In the long run, the best way to ensure that a finite goal remains finite is by avoiding the behaviors that can make a Type A feel he's facing an open-ended sky-high goal, such as comparisons ("I know your goal on the test was a B, but your friend Tommy got a B-plus and I know you can do better than him") or open-ended praise ("You achieved your goal so quickly that I think you can do even better").

### STAGE TWO: IMPLEMENTING THE GOAL

On my office wall hangs a cartoon of a boy riding a bike. He is about 9 or 10, has a Bart Simpson spike haircut, and his smile is a mile wide. The most notable thing about him, though, is the reckless way he's riding his bike. Instead of gripping the handlebars, his arms are spread out winglike at his sides, and instead of facing forward, his head is turned backward at a 90-degree angle toward his mother, who is standing behind him looking horrified because she can see what he can't: he is about to crash into the family garage.

In the course of an average week, I refer to this cartoon at least once or twice, and usually it's in the presence of a parent who looks just as horrified as the mother in the cartoon. Watching their Type A child pursue a goal is often a hair-raising experience for parents. Children—even unusually intelligent children—still have the world partly upside down, and this topsy-turvy outlook frequently is reflected in the way they pursue a goal. The child will insist on doing X, when Y is clearly the best way to achieve the goal; or on doing C, even though C is inefficient and time-consuming.

It's usually after a parent has described one of these topsy-turvy choices that I mention the cartoon. Then I tell him or her, "I sympathize with your upset, but the best way to help your child is by doing what you're already doing—nothing."

Invariably, this statement comes as a surprise. But nine out of ten times, doing nothing is the best parental strategy for this stage of the goal process. One of the most important experiences a parent can provide a goal-pursuing child is the freedom to make mistakes and fail. I know this sounds paradoxical, but standing back and giving the Type A—or any youngster, for that matter—the freedom to make and implement his own plans sends the self-esteem-boosting message, "I trust you to figure out how to do this." Equally important, it also provides him with an unparalleled opportunity to learn. No matter how many times you say, "This is the right way to do it," the child will remember the right way better if he's allowed to discover it on his own by making a plan, seeing it go awry, and then correcting his mistakes.

Admittedly, watching a Type A flounder around like a Keystone Cop during the learning process can be difficult, particularly if, like Barbara Cullen, the parent is a Type A with strong directive impulses. But as Barbara discovered with a little help from me, the parent who gives her chld floundering room almost always is rewarded in the end for her patience.

Barbara's travail began last January when her daughter Beth implemented her New Year's goal—getting a part-time job. What upset Barbara wasn't the job; she and Beth both agreed it was a good idea. However, it had an unexpected and devastating impact on Beth's grades. From January through late April, Beth's GPA sank like a stone—from her usual B-plus, to a B, then a C-plus, and finally, in the last weeks of April, to a C. The reason I remember these milestones so clearly is that during this period, Barbara and I talked a great deal.

When Beth's GPA dropped to a B, she began calling me regularly. In the period when it hovered between C-plus and C, we were in contact almost daily. Through all these conversations, my counsel to Barbara was the same—patience. I was sure Beth was encountering the U-curve phenomenon that frequently develops when a goal is first pursued. As the youngster experiments with various methods of implementing a goal his performance drops; then, when he finds the right method, it begins rising again.

And so it was with Beth.

Like many teenagers with first-time jobs, Beth didn't know much about budgeting her time. Also like many teenagers with new jobs, her inexperience initially produced some bad choices: Beth's decision to reduce her weekly studying time from twelve hours to seven; to continue socializing five nights a week; and to insist on working twenty-five rather than twenty hours per week. But also like many teenagers, Beth proved capable of learning from her mistakes. By mid-April, she was experimenting with a new formula: more studying time and a little less work and socializing time. By May, this was proving to be a winning formula. Beth's grades had begun climbing the ascending side of the U.

One characteristic of a good goal is that it teaches a child a little more than was intended. In Beth's case, these lessons were twofold. She learned a lesson about time budgeting that will stay with her the rest of her life, and she learned a lesson about her mother's confidence in her, which will also stay with her the rest of her life.

What if, as sometimes happens, the child asks for help in implementing a goal?

This is an exception to the do-nothing rule. If Beth had asked her mother for help in scheduling her time, it would have been perfectly appropriate for Barbara to provide it. Another exception to the do-nothing rule is when the Type A's mistakes make him so nervous that it affects his ability to pursue the goal. Typically, the child who falls victim to this kind of performance anxiety has trouble sleeping, begins obsessing about the maddeningly elusive goal, and, most telling of all, his increasingly frantic efforts to achieve it produce increasingly meager results.

In sports terminology, this last phenomenon is known as "the choke." Anxiety about doing well becomes so overwhelming that it inhibits the youngster's ability to act and think clearly.

Explaining what's happening sometimes helps. If the Type A understands the source of his problem and has learned the stress reduction strategies in chapter 12, he may be able to conquer his anxiety and go on to attain the goal. But if, despite his and your best efforts, he continues to stumble, the best policy is to declare the goal null and void.

The failure will disappoint him, but there are a number of ways to assuage this disappointment. They bring us to stage three in the goal process.

STAGE THREE: HELPING THE TYPE A COME TO TERMS WITH
A FAILED GOAL

For a child who, like Chicken Little, is inclined to view even the smallest setback as a sign that the sky is falling, failure is a crushing blow. No matter how insignificant, it leaves the Type A feeling small and humiliated. And a Type A in his unhappy frame of mind will make not only himself miserable but those around him, particularly if he secretly holds them responsible for his failure. Simon Lindquist is a good example of this point.

How Simon became so angry at his father, Peter, is a long and complex story, and one also full of good parental intentions. Last March, when Simon mentioned his plan to organize a summer lawn-mowing business, Peter was supportive and encouraging. But, being a Type A with a high personal-achievement need, Peter's supportiveness and encouragement got away from him. As is so often the case, the result was a sky-high goal. Instead of a modest service of twenty or twenty-five customers—Simon's original plan—Peter said, "Sign up forty or fifty customers." Instead of limiting the service just to lawns—also Simon's original intention—Peter said, "Include shrubbery."

A clear line can be drawn between the disaster that followed and the new gash in Peter's car. By the end of the summer, more than half of Simon's original customers had canceled. The remaining ones were so unhappy with their overtired, overextended, inexperienced lawn man that bill collection became a real problem. Had Peter known how to talk to Simon about his disappointment, or had he known how to do any of the other things a parent needs to do when his child's goal fails, Simon might not have felt so angry. But Peter didn't know, and Simon was left to stew in his anger. The more he stewed, the more he found himself thinking about his father and especially about his dad's new BMW. One night in early November, he said to Peter, "Why don't you let me park the car tonight?"

Simon insists that the resulting gash in the car was an accident, but experience would indicate that it was a form of acting out by an angry teenager.

In fairness to Peter Lindquist, I should point out that such parental knowledge gaps are common and understandable in Type A homes. After all, how do you help a child handle failure when success means so much to him?

Following are six strategies that will help restore the disappointed A's confidence in himself and in those around him.

**Step A:** *Encourage the defeated A to talk about his pain and disappointment.* You do this by being a sympathetic listener. I'll have much more to say about this in chapter 9, but there are two aspects of being a good listener that are pertinent here. The first is that he knows not to deal with his child's failure by immediately praising or immediately reassuring him. Often, these are a parent's first impulses when a goal fails, and they are understandable ones. It hurts to see someone you love in pain. But immediate praise and reassurance often have the unintended effect of making the child feel worse than he already does—partly because praise sounds hollow after a defeat ("Mom, I just struck out. What's so terrific?"), and partly because both praise and immediate reassurance often have the unintended effect of making the child think his feelings are being denied. In the child's mind, "Well, I think that was good," is translated as, "Well, Mom and Dad don't want to hear how I feel about failure."

Parental reassurance, and sometimes praise, are in order after defeats and failures—but later on.

The other thing a sympathetic listener knows is that unvoiced feelings have a way of building until they get so big that they produce explosions like the one that left a dent in Peter Lindquist's BMW. So, a good listener always gives his defeated child all the time and room he needs to talk about his disappointment, anger, and frustration. Even when friends Bobby and Ned are dragged in out of the blue and made agents of a defeat, he still lets his child ventilate uninterruptedly, because he knows that the more his child talks about Bobby or Ned, the less likely he will be to make them targets of his acting out.

As with praise and reassurance, unfair finger-pointing should be corrected, but later, after the Type A has had an opportunity to ventilate his feelings.

Step B: *Tell your Type A about a childhood failure or defeat that made you feel the way he's feeling now.* One of the things which make setbacks and defeats so crushing for a child is a lack of perspective. The Type A child thinks no one has ever failed the way he's just failed or felt as bad about a failure as he feels at this moment. The point of telling stories about yourself, which is basically what this step involves, is to show the youngster that his experience isn't unusual; you have been there, too. In addition, your stories make a subtle point about surviving failure. If you picked yourself up after yours, he can pick himself up after his.

This strategy is also a wonderful vehicle for parent-child bonding. I don't think my son Matt and I have ever felt closer than the afternoon I told him about a childhood defeat of mine. What prompted me to share it was the collapse of one of Matt's cherished adolescent goals.

"I know just how you feel," I said, the day Matt told me he'd been cut from his school's baseball squad. And I did. Never had I felt so inept or disappointed in myself as I did on the June day in 1954 when, at 9 years old, I stood on the pitcher's mound at Severelli Park in New York City and surveyed the damage I had inflicted on my team in the first half-inning of my Little League debut. I'd already surrendered nine runs; I had three men on base, and I'd yet to get my first out. As I watched my next pitch sail into the cloudless summer sky, I thought of a movie I had seen recently, *High Noon*, and decided that the only person who could know how vulnerable and alone I felt at that awful moment was Gary Cooper's character as he walked down the deserted street to meet the three gunmen waiting at the other end. Certainly my coach couldn't know; otherwise he wouldn't have left me in until the bitter end of the inning (by which time I'd surrendered fifteen runs). Nor could my poor, perplexed mother, who knew something awful was happening to her son but didn't know enough about baseball to know what it was; nor my older cousin, who was too happy thinking about how he would be able to use this humiliation to torture me for the next half-dozen years.

On occasion, Matt isn't above tweaking my nose with this story. But sharing it with him the afternoon of his defeat did more than just make his own disappointment more bearable; it also introduced him to a figure he hadn't met before—the confused, frightened 9-year-old his father once had been. I think that, having met him, Matt now finds it easier to approach me when he has a problem or wants advice, or when he just wants someone to listen as he talks about his hopes and dreams for his future.

Step C: *Point out to your Type A all the things he's accomplished while pursuing his goal.* No failure is ever total. In trying to achieve a goal, a child takes on many new challenges, and even if he doesn't meet every one, chances are that he will meet some of them. Implementing this strategy means reviewing these challenges with the child, praising him for those he has met, and pointing out what was learned from those unmet. This kind of discussion has the same effect as step B, telling stories about yourself. It's a way of teaching the youngsters how to do something very few children can do on their own: put a failure into perspective.

Listening to you describe how thoughtful it was to do X or explain how much he learned from Y, even though Y didn't work out quite as planned, the child thinks, "Yes, that's right, I did some things I didn't think I could do, and I also learned a lot."

For instance, the day Simon told me about the collapse of his lawn service, his ego was in even worse shape than the injured forehead that prompted his visit. After I finished stitching the gash on it, I suggested we have a talk. "I know you're feeling pretty bad about yourself now," I said, as I handed him a Coke and directed him to my couch, "but if you stop and think about it, Simon, you've accomplished quite a bit this summer."

Simon looked at me like I had just grown another head.

Undaunted, I pointed out that he had signed up over forty customers for his service and managed to do it within six weeks, and for a business without any previous track record. "How many sixteen-year-olds do you think could manage that?" I said. I also pointed out that even though the lawn service hadn't been the success Simon had hoped, it had taught him a lot about running a business.

I won't say Simon left my office with a song in his heart, but I do think our talk gave him a new perspective on his business venture. If it hadn't been the success he and his father had wanted it to be, it wasn't the unmitigated disaster it appeared to be, either. Simon had scored some major successes and learned some important things.

Step D: *Help the Type A child problem-solve for the next time.* Because of the special associations failure carries, the Type A won't surrender easily to it. If a goal didn't work out the first time, often he'll press and cajole for a second try. This creates a dilemma for the parent. Should another effort be encouraged, even though the failure may further damage the child's self-esteem? If the failure is the result of a goal that proved beyond the child's ability, I believe "no" is the appropriate answer to this question. (We'll look at how to prevent a Type A from fixating on a failed goal in the next step.) But if it was due to poor planning, as many childhood failures are, "yes" is appropriate, provided that the child is willing to sit down with his parent and analyze why his pursuit of the goal failed.

The point of this analysis is to help the Type A identify where he went wrong and what he needs to do to correct his mistake. Such knowledge can make a big difference, as Jeannie Acton discovered last year when she and her father spent some time analyzing why her primary freshman-year goal—extending her circle of friends—failed.

Even for the academic-minded Type A, social goals are *very* important. As Jeannie and her father analyzed the reasons for the failure of her eminently achievable social goal, several conclusions suggested themselves. They decided that it was very likely that Jeannie's habit of being supercritical had scared off some potential new friends. Her tendency to be brusque and impatient, and her need to get her own way, may have put off others. The results of this analysis not only make it more likely that Jeannie's sophomore year will be more social than her freshman year was, but the analysis taught her a few important lessons about herself.

Step E: *Prevent the Type A child from getting stuck on his failure.* If parent and child decide that a failed goal shouldn't be pursued, the best thing for the child to do is to put the failure behind him. But this is especially hard for the Type A youngster, whose insecurities give failure a Velcro-like effect. Weeks or even months later, the A is still stuck on the catch he missed, the grade he didn't get, the election he lost, or the business that failed. The most effective way to get him unstuck is to help him find a new success, so that he'll have something new to think about (and you, something new to listen to).

One way to find a new success is to use the skills you learned in Stage One to help create an alternative goal that gives him some of the satisfactions he sought in the failed goal. Another is to try to steer the youngster in an entirely new direction. This alternative is most appropriate when the child feels burned out by a failure.

For example, the last thing Simon Lindquist wanted to do at the end of last summer was to start a new business. And the last thing Peter Yin wanted to do after he failed to win the first-violin position in the Westchester County Orchestra was to try out for his high school's orchestra.

"I want to get away from music for a while," Peter replied when his father, David, made this suggestion. The refusal threw David, who is a professional musician. Music is an integral part of his and Peter's life. He couldn't think of an alternative goal that didn't involve it. However, I could. When David called me for advice, I suggested he talk to Peter about joining the school newspaper.

"I know Peter hasn't shown any interest in journalism," I said. "But I think it will satisfy many of the same impulses that draw him to music. Journalism is also a collaborative effort, and it requires the same type of intensity and concentration as music. I suspect you'll find Peter takes to it readily." And indeed Peter did. Although he never made first violin in our All-County Orchestra, by the end of the school year Peter felt he had compensated for that defeat by being chosen assistant editor for the next year.

Step F: *Have the Type A share with peers his hurt feelings about a failed goal.* No matter how sensitive or understanding a parent may be about a failure, the age difference makes it hard for her to console her child the way a peer can. I know that was true for me after my Little League debacle. The night it happened, my father had many wise things to say to me, and my mother, even more. But nothing they said made me feel quite as good—or perhaps more accurately, relieved—as a conversation I had at the next game with my team's shortstop. The boy, whom I'd only met a few weeks earlier, knew very little about me as an individual, and nothing about the psychology of comforting. But he did know what it felt like to be 9 years old, and to feel you have just committed the greatest blunder in history. This "kid" knowledge oozed through in every syllable of every word he said to me that day. After our conversation, for the first time in a week I felt I could hold my head up.

You won't always be able to find someone as empathetic as my shortstop, but if you know another child who has suffered a similar defeat, try to get him together with your Type A child. They will have a lot to talk about.

# 9

# How to Talk to a Type A Child

Two snippets of typical parent–Type A child dialogue:

CHILD: I'm disappointed.
PARENT: What's the matter?
CHILD: I only got a B-plus on that geometry test.
PARENT: A B-plus! That's terrific!
CHILD: No, it's not! The test was a breeze. I should have done better. I'm disappointed.
PARENT: Oh, don't feel disappointed. I have an idea that will cheer you up. Why don't you think about the camping trip we're taking this weekend?

CHILD: I hate Mrs. Levine.
PARENT: Your teacher?
CHILD: She's a real creep. She sent me out of the class today for talking.
PARENT: Well, maybe you were being disruptive. I know Mrs. Levine. She's a wonderful teacher.
CHILD: Yeah, well, I'd like to tie her to a stake and burn her. I really hate her.
PARENT: Look, if you want to dislike Mrs. Levine, that's your right. But we don't hate people in this house. Hate is an ugly emotion.

**134**

Both of these parents sound thoughtful and sensitive, and both want to be. But at a certain point in these dialogues, both misstep, and in the same way. Each rejects a feeling the child has, and then imposes his or her own point of view. The father in the first dialogue does it by telling his disappointed Type A to "cheer up"; the mother in the second, by telling hers that hate is an unacceptable emotion.

Studies show that the form of communication these parents used, which I call *parent-centered*, is very common in Type A homes. It usually arises almost as a defensive reaction. Strong and willful, impatient and impetuous, Type A's are full of so many troubling or unreasonable thoughts and feelings that often when a parent talks to a Type A, he feels he has to do what the parents in the dialogues did—impose his point of view on the A.

This tendency to impose the parental point of view by telling the child what he should think, feel, or believe is *the* defining characteristic of parent-centered communication. To help you understand why it also promotes negative Type A behavior, I'm going to ask you to do some perspective taking. Imagine that you're at a meeting where you and four other people are exchanging ideas and opinions, except that every time you offer a thought or opinion, someone immediately corrects, admonishes, or otherwise interrupts you.

If you are like most people, you will probably leave the meeting feeling bad about yourself (if your colleagues think so little of your ideas that they keep interrupting you, they probably don't think much of you either) and also angry, even hostile (how dare they treat you so thoughtlessly?). In other words, you will leave the meeting a little more Type A than you were before it began.

Child-centered communication, the subject of this chapter, is designed to ensure that parent-child conversations don't have the same effect on the Type A. Such communication recognizes that Type A's need a great deal of parental guidance and counseling, but it also recognizes that for parent-child communication to be the building block of self-esteem that it should be, the Type A also has to feel that his thoughts and feelings are *always* accepted.

I know many of you are thinking, "Uh-oh. Dr. Shelov is about to tell me the next time my Type A comes home and announces that his friend Steven is 'stupid' or worse, the next time he comes home and announces, 'I'm stupid,' I'll have to agree."

I'm not.

Parental agreement isn't necessary to make a child feel that his thoughts and feelings are accepted. All you have to do is:

• Give him an opportunity to explain without correcting, admonishing, praising, or otherwise interrupting him.
• If criticism is necessary, criticize him in a way that says, "I accept your right to hold a different opinion from mine."

These two steps are the key building blocks of child-centered communication. As you master them, you will find that they not only make your Type A feel better about himself, but they change the nature of communication in your home.

Child-centered communication increases the A's willingness to really listen when you offer advice, counsel, or comfort. A major reason why many Type A's don't listen is that they don't get what a child needs before he can listen—an opportunity to ventilate urgent thoughts and feelings.

In time, however, child-centered communication also produces another, even bigger change. Few things are more enjoyable to a child than knowing that his thoughts and feelings are respected and accepted. When he finds a listener ready to extend that acceptance and respect, he'll turn to her again and again—not just when he has a problem or wants advice, but when he wants someone to listen to his hopes and dreams.

Here's how child-centered communication works.

### SKILL ONE: HOW TO LISTEN

This skill is built upon the need for parental acceptance.

#### *Listening When Your Child Knows What He Wants to Say*

To understand why this form of listening is important to your Type A, I'm going to ask you to do another bit of perspective taking. Imagine something terrible happened today: You were fired. This is a crushing experience, and by the time you sit down to dinner, you are bursting with a thousand conflicting and irrational emotions. You feel angry, wronged, incompetent, confused, and vengeful. You know you're not thinking clearly, and you also know your spouse can help restore you to rationality. But if you're like most people, you also know that before you can listen to your spouse, you have to ventilate all those irrational and contradictory thoughts and feelings.

The 10-year-old Type A who wants to burn his teacher, Mrs. Levine at the stake feels the same way. Once he's ventilated his anger at her, he will be ready to hear parental counsel and advice. But first he wants and needs to ventilate. So, the first step in parental listening involves temporarily suspending the impulse to advise, counsel, and instruct. For the moment, you should simply accept what the child has to say.

Sometimes accepting is all you have to do. But often a youngster will want to be assured that you're not secretly judging, correcting, or chastising him for what he's saying. The best way to show that you're simply accepting what he's saying through a technique called paraphrasing. Essentially, it means summing up the concern the child is expressing and restating it to him, as in these examples:

CHILD: I wish I didn't have a math test tomorrow. I didn't get a chance to do much studying.
PARENT: So, you don't feel prepared for the test.
—or—
CHILD: I thought that movie was dumb.
PARENT: Oh, yeah, why did you think it was dumb?

I know that to adult ears such repetitions may sound contrived, even a little simple-minded. But when used judiciously—and by that I mean not after every sentence, but during conversational pauses—paraphrasing not only sends a message of parental acceptance ("Hey, Mom didn't tell me I should have studied for the test"), it also assures the child you're listening closely enough to identify his concerns (and if you've listened to as many parent-child conversations as I have, you'll understand why many youngsters want this reassurance).

The process just described may sound easy: you just accept what you hear and, on occasion, echo it back. But in Type A homes, uninterrupted listening rarely is easy. In part this is because the high incidence of overpraise, overcriticism, and overcomparison in such homes makes even temporary accept- ance hard. Also, the A's larger-than-life thoughts and feelings make many of the things he says hard to accept, even for the most accepting parent.

Consequently, such homes are much more prone to the listen- ing traps that break the circle of parent-child understanding. The child says something so unacceptably wrong, mean, outra- geous, sad, or troubling that the listening parent imposes her point of view in the form of an immediate correction, admoni- tion, or reassurance. A case in point is the parent in my first dialogue, who fell victim to the *bucking-up* trap. Instead of accepting his child's disappointment by letting him ventilate it, he immediately injected his point of view into the conversation by admonishing the child to cheer up.

In *disapproval*, a second common listening trap, the child is told very forthrightly that his thought or feeling or opinion is unacceptable. Usually this trap is triggered by the high-strung Type A's penchant for strong words. He'll say that something is "stupid" or "dumb" or announce that he "hates" or "loathes" a friend. Like the mother in my second example, a parent injects her point of view into the conversation by announcing that this thought or feeling is "unacceptable to me."

I touched on the third common listening trap, *blind praise and reassurance*, in chapter 8. The child says something so heart- breakingly sad that the parent feels it would be almost cruel just to accept it. So, instead of giving the youngster the oppor- tunity to explain why he feels sad, she responds by reminding him of all his good qualities or all the reasons he has to feel good about himself.

Now that you have an idea of how the listening traps work, let's see if you can avoid two other common ones. Imagine that your daughter marches into the living room and, with typical Type A hyperbole, announces that her friend Alexis is "pathetic. All she does is complain." Which reply tells her you are ready to be an accepting listener?

   1. "Alexis is a nice girl; you shouldn't talk about her that way."

2. "Honey, you're entitled to your feelings about Alexis, but I think a good rule is, 'If you can't say something nice about a person, don't say anything at all.'"
3. "You don't like Alexis anymore; you think she complains too much."

Number 3 is the correct reply. It accurately summarizes the child's feelings about Alexis and tells her you are ready to listen without interrupting while she describes them in detail. Replies 1 and 2 are examples of a trap I call *civilized discourse,* which arises from the justifiable and widely held parental belief that it is unacceptable to talk about friends in certain ways.

Let's see if you can spot the fifth listening trap. In this case, imagine the Alexis situation is reversed. Your Type A child comes home and says, "Alexis thinks I'm pathetic. She says I complain too much." Which reply signals you'll be an accepting listener?

1. "It sounds like Alexis's remark really upset you."
2. "Boy, friends can be mean sometimes. But look, I have an idea. I'm going to the mall this afternoon. Why don't you come with me? You want a new dress for the Halloween party. Maybe we can find one."

The first reply is the correct choice; it correctly paraphrases the child's statement about Alexis. Number 2 is an example of a trap I call *diversion;* it arises from the same impulse as bucking up and blind praise. Instead of accepting the youngster's pain by giving her room to describe it, the parent tries to assuage it; in the case of diversion, by bringing up a subject or suggesting an activity she knows the child likes.

At this point you may be thinking, "Wait a minute. Type A boys and girls often do and say things so unacceptable that a parental correction, admonition, or word of comfort is in order." You're right; they do. But, however justified and appropriate, when a parent inserts his point of view into the conversation *before* the child finishes explaining his, two things usually happen.

The first is that the Type A's (or indeed, any child's) self-esteem is damaged. An occasional overeager interruption or correction is not and should not be a source of parental concern. But if such interruptions are typical, communications become so parent-centered that the child finds he can rarely get past his second or third sentence without bumping up against the parent's point of view. In time, he may conclude, "I guess my thoughts and feelings are unacceptable." The child who reaches that conclusion is only a step away from also concluding, "I guess *I'm* unacceptable."

The other consequence of a too-hasty intervention is that you lose your chance to help. Your youngster could benefit from learning what you did when a childhood friend treated you as cruelly as Alexis just treated her, or why you think words like *dumb* or *stupid* or *hate* are inappropriate, or why you don't think it's a good idea to burn Mrs. Levine at the stake, or all the reasons you think he is wonderful. A too-hasty interruption closes off the opportunity to offer such comfort, counsel, or advice, because it makes the Type A conclude, "I guess no one wants to listen to me." And he will do what most of us do when we reach this conclusion: withdraw.

Just as you will be ready to listen to your spouse after you have ventilated all your feelings about being fired, your Type A child will be ready to listen to you after he has ventilated his concern—and not before.

Since parents vary in their vulnerability to the five listening traps, you and your spouse may want to divide listening chores according to what sets each of you off. For example, because expressions of hurt and sadness are especially painful to mothers, often they are more vulnerable to the blind reassurance and praise trap. So, if a big defeat or setback is to be discussed, Dad may be the more appropriate listener. On the other hand, men, being more authoritarian and win-minded, are especially vulnerable to the disapproval trap. So, if the subject of the conversation is likely to challenge paternal ideas about good and bad, right and wrong, or victory and defeat, Mom may be the best listener.

Since you won't always be present when your child needs a sympathetic listener, and since there are some things he won't want to discuss with you even if you are there, it's a good idea to have a few designated listeners who can be used as surrogates. A designated listener can be an uncle or aunt, or a coach, teacher, or guidance counselor. Recently I learned firsthand the importance of having such a listener in the school setting.

I was in my kitchen having a late dinner when my middle child, Sara, came in and asked me to sign a pink slip she had been given for a disciplinary infraction. The infraction was talking out of turn. This year, she and her best friend, Michella, have the same homeroom. Apparently, on this occasion the girls' propensity to chat got out of hand and Sara was sent to the guidance counselor's office.

Since the pink slip was a first for Sara, and since she is very serious about school, I was surprised by her attitude as she handed it to me.

"You look almost pleased," I said. "I would have thought you'd be pretty upset."

"I would have been, but Mrs. Di Napoli [the guidance counselor] was great."

"What did she do?" I asked.

"Nothing, she just listened."

At the next PTA meeting, I cornered Mrs. Di Napoli and told her about Sara's praise. She smiled and said:

"I think what Sara remembers is the first part of our conversation. I knew she wouldn't be ready to listen to me until I listened to her. So for the first ten minutes or so, I let her tell me why she felt Mrs. Crowley was unfairly picking on her and Michella. Then, I gave her Mrs. Crowley's side of the story."

One last point: If you are a Type A yourself, you may be prone to fidgety, impatient body language. Children are very sensitive to such language; they interpret it as a sign of parental disinterest, and it often makes them less forthcoming than they would otherwise be. Here are some body-language pointers that will assure your Type A that you are listening to him and that he is the most important thing on your mind right now.

*Always present a relaxed countenance.* This means keeping your arms and legs uncrossed, your facial expression open and nonjudgmental, and your gaze focused squarely on the child, instead of shifting it back and forth impatiently from him to another object in the room, as Type A parents often do.

*Position yourself on your child's level.* Instead of towering over him during conversation, make an effort to position yourself squarely in front of the youngster. You know you're in the right position when your eyes and shoulders are more or less on the same plane as your child's.

*Tilt your body forward.* This also makes an important statement to the child. Leaning forward says, "I'm interested."

*Create quiet.* While this isn't an aspect of body language (although a calm parental countenance does create a sense of quiet), another way to signal readiness to listen is to shut off the radio and TV and to eliminate all other noises when a child announces that he wants to talk.

SKILL TWO

### Listening When Your Child Doesn't Know What He Wants to Say

To illustrate why this more complex version of listening is important to your Type A, I'm going to ask you to do another bit of perspective taking. This time, I want you to put yourself in a situation I'm sure you've experienced several times. You are upset, but you don't know why. You know your fidgetiness signals anxiety, or that your sleeping difficulties indicate that you are depressed. Since emotions don't arise in a vacuum, you know something real is causing these feelings; but despite much earnest soul searching, you can't figure out what it is.

I call this phenomenon "hidden messages." For the most part, children and adults experience them the same way, but there are important differences. Being cognitively less mature, children have more hidden messages because they have more trouble identifying their concerns and upsets. Also, in a child, the emotions caused by hidden concerns usually are so much bigger and more upsetting that they frequently produce acting out, particularly in high-strung Type A's.

Simon Lindquist's putting a gash in his father's new BMW is one instance of acting out.

Another example is Danielle Michaud's contemptuous reaction to the $300 VCR her father, Rudy, bought her for Christmas. After a fifteen-second inspection, Danielle declared it "cheap and lousy." This remark confused Rudy, and me, when he told me about it, until Rudy also mentioned that Danielle's boyfriend had passed on an invitation to Christmas dinner at the Michauds' in favor of a football game.

The goal of this form of listening is to help a parent help his Type A identify and ventilate hidden messages such as, "What I really think is cheap and lousy is my boyfriend's behavior." It also builds the A's self-esteem through acceptance. But in this case, the acceptance required is broader. The parent not only has to accept the child's right to express (but *not* his right to act out) big, ugly, upsetting emotions instead of interrupting to criticize, correct, or admonish; he also has to accept the child's desire to want to discover the source of these emotions on his own.

This form of listening also casts the listener in a different role; he plays the part of a facilitator, who unobtrusively guides the child to his hidden messages by periodically—during conversational lapses or in moments of confusion—offering what are called "reflections." Like paraphrases, these are summations; except in this case, what's being summarized isn't content but emotion. The listening parent quite literally leaps over the confused child's words and reflects the emotions expressed in his words.

CHILD: I hate my bike.
PARENT: You sound angry.
*—or—*
CHILD: Billy says he can't come to the game Saturday.
PARENT: You sound sad.

I realize that reflection, like paraphrasing, may sound contrived, even manipulative. But to a confused child it serves two important functions. Emotionally, it reassures him that his right to explore his concerns at his own pace will be respected. Intellectually, it gets him thinking. Hearing a parent say, "You sound happy or sad or upset," makes the child say to himself, "Yes, I do feel that way. I wonder why." As the following dialogue illustrates, once a Type A begins asking himself that question, important revelations often follow.

CHILD: Mom, I got upset the other night when Laura came over.
PARENT: She made you nervous.
CHILD: You know, that's what it was. Laura's so popular at school. Everyone wants to be her friend.

PARENT: It sounds as if you really want Laura to like you.
CHILD: I do, I do. If the other kids know Laura likes me, they'll like me too. I don't have many friends now.
PARENT: Let's talk about that.

Each of these comments does what a good reflection should do: it unobtrusively focuses and refines the child's thinking on an important issue. The first helps her to understand why being with Laura is so anxiety-provoking: she wants to be Laura's friend. The second helps her to understand why that's so important: she hopes it will end her unpopularity. What makes the discovery process flow so smoothly in this dialogue is the absence of a threateningly parental point of view. The child is never rushed or told what to think. She is given the room to make her own discoveries at her own pace. Only after the last painful admission does the parent interject herself into the conversation, with a suggestion that they talk about the problem.

This form of listening also may sound easy, but in fact it's just as hard as the first kind, and for the same reason. Uncritical acceptance—even if it's only momentary—often is difficult in homes where there is a high incidence of overpraise and overencouragement, and of outrageous thoughts, feelings, and opinions. One consequence of this combination is that the reflecting parent is just as likely to fall into one of the listening traps as into the paraphrasing one.

A case in point is Rudy Michaud. Instead of temporarily accepting his daughter's anger about the VCR and reflecting it back in a statement like, "Boy, do you sound mad this morning," he stepped into the disapproval trap by snapping, "You have no right to talk to me like that, young lady." Given his daughter's strong language, Rudy's reaction was understandable, but his criticism brought the conversation—and his chance to help Danielle ventilate her pain about her boyfriend's behavior—to an end.

In addition to disapproval, diversion, bucking up, false praise, and reassurance, reflection-based listening has several traps unique to it. See if you can spot the first one.

Imagine that you and your son had a falling-out last night. While his friend Timmy was visiting, he acted disrespectful toward you; now, feeling guilty, he offers this apology: "Dad, I'm sorry I was so smart-alecky last night. But I always feel a little funny when Timmy starts talking about what a great football player he is." Which statement best reflects the emotion underneath this statement?

1. "You did seem upset last night."
2. "I understand that you feel bad. But Timmy must have a great arm. He said he completed four for four passes in the last game."

The first is the correct answer; the second is an example of a trap called "diverted by content." The child says something so interesting that the parent forgets about reflection and begins discussing that "interesting something" with him—as in "Timmy must have a great arm." Often, a listening parent has to pick up on the things a child says to keep the reflection process moving, but if he or she begins focusing solely or largely on content, at a certain point the youngster will feel that his real concerns are being ignored.

Now, imagine that your child says, "Gee, I wish I had more friends." Your answer is:

1. "You sound sad."
2. "You sound lonely."
3. "How does that make you feel?"

Number 3 is the correct answer; 1 and 2 are examples of the guessing trap. The child may be sad or lonely, but he also could be angry about his predicament. "I wish I had more friends," like many statements a child makes, is open to several possible emotional interpretations. When confronted with such ambiguity, the best thing to do is what the parent in reply 3 did: ask the child directly, "How do you feel about that?"

Here's the last listening trap common to reflecting parents. See if you can avoid it. Imagine that your child has just said, "I hate Maureen!" How should you reply?

1. "You sound angry at your sister."
2. "Boy, do you sound mad. I'll bet I know why. Maureen broke the arm off of one of your Teenage Mutant Ninja Turtles."

Since both statements accurately reflect the emotion expressed, both are correct. But number 2 represents an example of the *right-answer* trap. Rather than see the child flounder around in confusion, the parent tells him why he's angry. The impulse behind this behavior is understandable, but it often has an unfortunate consequence. It doesn't produce the sense of resolution that comes when the child pinpoints a nagging problem on his own. Lacking that sense, the child won't be in a mood to sit and listen when he is offered advice on how to handle his problem with Maureen.

There are two other things you need to know about reflection-based listening. The first is how to tell when you are dealing with a hidden message. Usually, if your Type A is harboring one, the emotions it produces will result in one of these forms of acting out:

- Uttering neutral or innocent statements with inappropriate anger, depression, or anxiety.
- Behaving in an uncharacteristic way. If he's normally a pacifist. he may suddenly begin picking fights; if he's normally fastidious, he may begin ignoring the state of his room.
- Using certain telling words repeatedly. Generally, the child who finds everything and everyone around him dumb, stupid, or horrible is secretly worried that *he* may be dumb, stupid, or horrible.
- Developing a weakness for non-sequiturs. Hidden messages often generate the kinds of feelings that lead to out-of-the-blue remarks such as, "Mom, Tommy says he can ride a two-wheeler now. You know what? I hate my bike!"

Another thing you need to know is what to do when reflections don't work. This happens at moments when the child doesn't feel like exploring his thoughts and feelings. This wish should be respected. You can come back to the topic later, when he's in a more reflective mood.

Sometimes, however, reflections don't provide enough guidance; the child needs more help ferreting out his hidden message. At such times, the parent should become an active participant. If you are dealing with a young Type A, try perspective taking. Tell him that if you were in his position, this is how you'd feel, and then name some emotions. With older children and adolescents, you can be more direct. Say, "I have some ideas about what may be going on, and you may, too. Why don't we kick them around for a while?"

If this effort fails, let the topic drop for the time being. You can come back to it later. In the meantime, talk to your spouse and see if he or she has any ideas about the child's hidden message.

### HOW TO CRITICIZE (AND PRAISE)

To illustrate why this skill also is a key building block of child-centered communication, I'm going to ask you once again to try some perspective taking. Imagine that your superior calls you into her office, closes the door, and picking up your marketing report from her desk, says, "This is terrible. I'm only on page four, and I've already found ten mistakes. What were you thinking when you wrote it? You're a bad employee." If you're like most people, you'll feel hurt, angry, diminished by her words. Someone you respect and admire, and who also has a lot of power over you, has just told you that you are unworthy.

Criticism makes the Type A child feel the same way, except that lacking your maturity, sense of perspective, and secure sense of self, he finds it even more anger-provoking and diminishing. Yet, children with vaunting ambitions and volatile temperaments often do need a great deal of criticism. This puts the A's parent in the difficult position of trying to square a circle.

How can she provide needed admonishment and correction, yet not provoke anger or a sense of unworthiness?

Again, the answer is parental acceptance. However, with criticism, this means accepting not only the A's right to his own perspective but his right to feel that bad behavior does not make him a bad child or diminish his good points. There are six strategies that make criticism child-, rather than parent-, centered.

Here's how each works:

*Preface criticism with point-of-view remarks.* Incorporating the chastised or scolded child's point of view into your criticism is a way of telling him, "While I disagree with you, I respect your right to think and feel the way you do." Examples of statements that send this message are: "You have a right to be angry at your sister, but . . ."; "I understand why you think organizing a paper route would be a good way to make money, but . . ."; and, "I know you feel grown-up enough to have an eleven-o'clock curfew, but . . ."

Because such prefaces preserve the child's respect, they also make him more receptive to the criticism that follows. A case in point is an experience I had with my son Eric when he was 6. One Saturday afternoon I arrived home to find him in the den watching *Jaws*. Actually, "hovering" would be a more accurate description of his state, since the anxiety the movie was generating seemed to have lifted him up and suspended him six inches above his chair.

I knew that if I said, "Eric, you shouldn't be watching *Jaws*, it's too scary for a six-year-old," he would not only feel diminished, but the criticism would make him resistant. So I offered the following point-of-view remark: "Eric, I know you think it takes a lot to scare you, but *Jaws* is a very, very scary movie; why don't you shut it off and we'll play Operation?" I won't say Eric leaped at my suggestion, but because my remark respected, rather than challenged, a belief he held about himself (scary movies don't scare me), he didn't resist it. After insisting that *Jaws* didn't scare him at all, he shut off the TV and took out Operation.

*Always be specific when criticizing.* Of all the critical traps parents fall into, global criticism, the one most damaging to self-esteem, is also the easiest to avoid. When a parent says, "You're bad," or, "You're sloppy," she knows she's referring to the slap the Type A gave his little sister, or the ten grammar errors in his book report. But because, in the heat of the critical moment, she fails to make this crucial distinction to the A, he walks away thinking that what's bad or sloppy isn't hitting his little sister or the ten errors in his book report, but he himself.

Being specific in criticism means making such distinctions clear to the child, as in these examples:

"I don't think it was a good idea to take that course," instead of, "You're too ambitious for your own good."

*Or:*

"I wish you wouldn't get so angry at your brother," instead of, "You're such an angry kid."

Both of these remarks leave a child in no doubt that he's been corrected, but because they focus on the transgression rather than the transgressor, the child is allowed to walk away thinking that while Mom and Dad may not like what he said or did, they still like him.

*Balance negative remarks with positive ones.* Letting a criticized child know that you never lose sight of his good qualities is another way of preserving his self-esteem. That is what you do when you make statements such as, "Why did you get angry at your brother? You're usually the family peacemaker," or "I'm surprised you decided to take that extra course; you're usually pretty sensible about budgeting your time," or "You made some excellent points in your book review, but I do think you could make them more clearly." Because each of these remarks provides praise as well as criticism, each allows the child to walk away feeling good both about himself and about his critic.

Since we all like to hear nice things about ourselves, such praise also makes the child more receptive to criticism and correction. I'm pretty confident that the other reason why Eric didn't resist my suggestion that we play Operation is because I also said, "I know a brave guy like you can handle *Jaws*, but . . ."

*Describe how a transgression or bad behavior makes you feel.* Prefacing critical remarks with parental expressions of feeling, such as, "I'm worried," or "I'm afraid," or "It upsets me," also preserves self-respect, because such expressions recast critical comments into statements of parental concern. Hearing "I'm worried," or "I'm upset," the child realizes that his behavior is objectionable, not because he's bad or mean but because his parent loves him and is afraid that if he persists in doing what he's doing, he may suffer a bad consequence.

Another advantage of using expressions of concern is that they introduce the Type A to empathy. While A's often spend a great deal of time thinking and complaining about how other people's behavior affects them, they rarely give much thought to the way their actions affect others. Remarks such as, "I'm worried" or "I'm concerned" are a good way of reminding them that their behavior does affect you.

*Explain why a criticism is necessary.* Once parental adrenaline starts flowing, it's hard to stop and patiently explain why the child's transgression is wrong. But the parent who maintains enough self-control to do this helps both the Type A and himself. The Type A is helped because the explanation shows him that his parents respect him enough to explain why his behavior is wrong; the parent is helped because the explanation makes the child receptive to criticism.

Youngsters are remarkably fair-minded. If they understand why a behavior is wrong, they will usually submit to a critique with a modicum of grace. But since 8-, 10-, and 12-year-olds often have trouble understanding why a missed curfew or a hypercompetitive attitude is wrong, before displaying that grace they have to have the consequence of the behavior spelled out to them.

*If possible, find an alternative to criticism.* A major reason for the high incidence of criticism in Type A homes is a lack of alternative ways to deal with problematic situations. The A sets an impossibly high goal for himself or makes a nasty comment about a friend or breaks a promise, and the parent criticizes him because she doesn't know any other way of handling the situation.

At times, there are other ways of making your point. An example is a strategy I call "countering with an alternative." Say that your Type A child comes up with a plan or goal you consider unrealistic. Countering with a more realistic plan or goal allows you to make your point—"I consider this a bad idea"—but without criticism. "Say it with a word" does the same thing. Pointing to the family dog and saying, "The dog," or to an unkempt room and saying, "Luke, your room," lets Luke know in no uncertain terms how unhappy you are about his broken promise to keep his room neat or walk the dog each morning—but, again, without criticism. This is also the goal of a strategy I call "providing information." The parent who uses it acts as a sort of teacher. For example, if the Type A's room is littered with books or clothes, instead of saying, "What a mess; pick that up immediately," she instructs by reminding him, "Books belong on the shelves, and clothes in the closet." Or, if the child wants an eleven-o'clock weekend curfew, instead of saying, "No, you're too young," she points out that a lot of dangerous things can happen to 13- or 14-year-olds who are walking the streets at eleven o'clock on a Friday or Saturday night.

One last point: A lot of the Type A's transgressions will be annoying. Don't be afraid to let your feelings show when you criticize. If the transgression is really serious, it's appropriate to raise your voice. Trying to be nice when you are smoldering inside will make the object of your criticism think you're being emotionally dishonest with him. It will also set you up, since, if you are really angry, chances are you will end up acting out your anger in a way that may leave the child feeling baffled and hurt.

It's just as important not to let yourself get out of control. If you find yourself very angry, it may be best to tell your child, "I'm so mad now, I can't talk to you." This isn't the best way to end a parent-child conversation, but it shows your child that you have such regard for him, you don't want to blow up at him.

A few words about praise:

Child-centered praise also involves acceptance, but in this case the acceptance is of the child's need and desire for parental approval and commendation. The parents of every Type A should want to meet this need. The goal of the three strategies below is to help you to meet it without unwittingly transforming your praise into a sky-high goal.

*Describe an accomplishment rather than use superlatives to praise it.* This, the key rule of praise, often baffles parents. You can understand how global criticisms such as, "You're bad," or, "You're wrong," can be damaging, but how can such resonant, affirmative superlatives as "terrific," "wonderful," and "great" be damaging to a child's self-esteem? Studies suggest there are several answers to this question.

One is that global superlatives such as "great" and "terrific" often are deeply threatening to a child because of the high standard of expectation they impose. "I may have been terrific today," the A thinks, "but what about the next time?" A not infrequent by-product of this worry is the familiar Type A performance anxiety, and a not infrequent by-product of that anxiety is that, when the next time rolls around, the child is so anxious about doing terrifically that he fails.

Depending on how they are used, global superlatives also can seem like a polite form of dismissal. Even a 5-year-old can figure out what's going on when a parent praises a drawing as "wonderful," then promptly returns to her cooking or her book. She is using her superlatives to get rid of him. A not infrequent consequence of this experience is the Type A thought, "If I want to win Mom's attention [and, by implication, love], next time I'm going to have to try harder to impress her."

A third danger of superlatives is that they often are experienced as a form of manipulation. Hearing himself praised to the heavens, the youngster begins to wonder whether Mom and Dad really mean it or whether the praise is part of larger parental plans to get him to do something he doesn't want to do.

Descriptive praise means describing to a child why you are impressed by his accomplishments, as in these examples:

"You know what I liked best about your picture? The way you drew the house. You got the floor and chimneys and doors just right. And oh, look, you even drew a nice tree next to the house."

*Or:*

"I really like your paper on pollution, particularly the part about the danger of toxic waste. You must have put a lot of time and effort into the research."

These statements work for a Type A for all the reasons that superlatives don't work. Because they are specific, they show him that the praiser was sufficiently impressed by his achievement to notice and savor its fine points. And because they are also very concrete, they avoid the flights into hyperbole that can leave the object of praise feeling threatened or manipulated.

*Find a word that sums up your praise.* Praising the author who showed such perseverance in researching his paper on pollution as "diligent" is one example of this strategy; praising the artist who drew such an eye-catching house as "imaginative" is another. Both of these statements give the child new, positive ways to think about himself. As he hears his behavior summed up in words such as *thoughtful* or *brave* or *responsible* or *good friend*, he begins to incorporate these qualities into his self-image. "Yes," he thinks, "that's what I am." Over time, these positive qualities will begin to drive out the negative ones that cloud the Type A's self-image. In other words, when he thinks of himself now, he'll no longer think of an argumentative or aggressive child, but of the thoughtful, responsible youngster he hears described by his parents.

*Limit praise to the here and now.* This rule is designed to protect against projection, a phenomenon I've discussed several times in this book. In praising an achievement, the parent projects into the future by saying, in one form or another, "This is good, but I think you can do better next time." Sticking to the achievement under discussion, and only to it, is the best way of avoiding this form of sky-high goal-setting.

# 10

# Teaching the Type A Child Right from Wrong: Respect-Oriented Discipline

Bobby O'Donnell, age 8, knows many things. He knows the signal color of each Teenage Mutant Ninja Turtle, the batting average of every New York Met, and the name of nearly every sit-com character on TV. But there is one big thing Bobby doesn't know: how to tell right from wrong. And this moral blind spot has made Anna O'Donnell a frequent visitor at his elementary school. Anna was there twice during Bobby's first-grade year to discuss disciplinary infractions, and three times the following year for the same reason. But none of the things Anna heard during those visits were nearly as upsetting as the story she heard during her most recent visit to her son's school.

While the principal and assistant principal looked on, a classmate identified Bobby as the ringleader of a clique that sometimes used strongarm tactics to impose its members' wishes on other children. According to the accuser, clique members considered themselves an elite within the school, and woe be to the child who didn't accord them the deference they expected.

What brought the clique's existence to light and Bobby's problems with right and wrong to a head was his behavior in a school assembly. Miffed that the accuser was in an auditorium seat he wanted, Bobby asked him to move. The boy refused.

Later, Bobby and two other clique members cornered him in the schoolyard and threatened him. Fifteen minutes after that, the frightened boy was in the principal's office, describing Bobby's threats to the principal.

What most troubled Anna O'Donnell about the incident was her son's lack of remorse. At the conference, Bobby had been appropriately apologetic and contrite. But later that night, discussing it among themselves, he all but came out and said, "I don't think I did anything wrong. If I wanted the auditorium seat, why shouldn't I have it?"

Such moral myopia is not uncommon among Type A's. One of the first things researchers noticed when they began studying adult A's in the late 1950s was that a great many of them had a weakness for moral corner-cutting and like Bobby, saw nothing wrong in the practice. If a questionable behavior produced a desired result, that usually justified its use. At the time, the origins of this moral myopia were unclear, but recent research suggests it arises largely from the disciplining style employed in many Type A homes.

It's called "authoritarian," and you can get a pretty good idea of how it operates from the results of a recent study by Stanford psychologist Paul Bracke. Dr. Bracke found that compared to other children, misbehaving Type A's in general, and misbehaving Type A boys in particular, are much more likely to be spanked, hit, yelled at, or threatened, and much less likely to be told why a behavior is wrong or given a punishment tailored to its degree of wrongness.

How these disciplinary practices contribute to the Type A's moral myopia can be explained by the following: Yelling, threatening, and hitting make a child feel bad about himself; and it's axiomatic that a child who doesn't like or respect himself doesn't like or respect others. This means that he's less likely to care whether he harms, injures, cheats, or undermines others.

Another problem with authoritarian discipline is that it generates a great deal of anger and hostility. You are already familiar with the physical dangers these emotions pose to the Type A, but recent research suggests they also pose a moral danger. The unreasonable and humiliating imposition of parental authority makes the Type A so angry that he loses the mental clarity and inclination to do what a child needs to do to develop a firm sense of right and wrong: spend some time thinking about why a misbehavior might have harmful consequences for him or for someone else.

Uniformly harsh—and unexplained—punishments also add to the A's moral myopia by confusing him. Because nothing is explained, and every infraction is disciplined with the same severity, he often doesn't have the slightest idea why misbehavior X is more serious than misbehavior Y, and Y more serious than misbehavior Z.

In terms of moral development, respect-oriented discipline works for all the reasons authoritarian discipline doesn't. Because it always leaves the disciplined child feeling as if he is respected, it fosters the kind of high self-esteem that makes the A like and respect not only himself but others, too. And because it employs logical and tailored punishment, it eliminates the anger, hostility, and confusion that can impair his ability to think through the consequences of misbehavior.

What respect-oriented discipline doesn't do, however, is tell a parent which behaviors deserve punishment. I want to spend a moment on that subject because a parent whose ideas about right and wrong lack definition and conviction will equivocate in disciplinary situations.

Such equivocation can draw a parent into a power struggle. Children, and in particular Type A children, possess a sort of X-ray vision. When they sense that a parent isn't behind a disciplinary rule heart and soul, they will test, bait, and bully until she backs down. The other danger of waffling is that, in time, it can lead to an outright flaunting of parental authority. Because the disciplining parent is perceived as a paper tiger, the Type A thinks, "What the heck, I'll do it anyway. What's the worst she can do to me?"

Like beauty, misbehaviors reside in the eye of the beholder. But there are certain behaviors and attitudes every parent considers wrong, dangerous, or inappropriate. Identifying them beforehand will give your "no's" the kind of conviction that doesn't invite testing or challenging.

Now, let's turn to the two skills that make up respect-oriented discipline.

SKILL ONE: PREVENTIVE DISCIPLINE

The primary goal of this skill is to preserve and promote self-esteem, and it does it in two ways. One is by reducing the incidence of provocative disciplinary infractions by showing you how to prevent such infractions. The other is by showing you how to say "don't" in a way that also says "I respect you."

Here's how the skill works:

*Provide alternative behaviors.* A great many of the disciplinary infractions that set off parents occur because the Type A is placed in a difficult situation without the coping skills needed to manage it. Six-year-old Diedre Falk's supermarket antics offer a case in point. For the most part, Diedre's habit of grabbing boxes and cans off of shelves was propelled by simple boredom. Supermarkets don't hold much interest for an energetic, inquisitive 6-year-old, and without anything to engage or stimulate her on shopping expeditions, Diedre bored quickly. The more bored she became, the more likely she was to engage in the misbehavior, which would produce a threat or shout from her mother, Beverly Falk. Usually, the endpoint of this unhappy scenario was anguish for both parties. Diedre would be reduced to tears by her mother's behavior, and Beverly to a state of acute guilt and embarrassment over her public loss of control.

Alternative behaviors are based on the premise that in difficult situations even a high-strung child won't succumb to mischief-producing anger, boredom, frustration, or impatience if he's provided with something absorbing to do. And exhibit A of the strategy's effectiveness is Diedre Falk. I won't say that the supermarket manager now leaps with joy when he sees the Falks enter his store. But ever since Diedre has been assigned her own shopping chores (fruits and snacks), she is too preoccupied to cause the kind of mischief that used to set off Beverly.

Ira Burrows also has found alternative behaviors an effective way to short-circuit a practice that used to play into his weakness for yelling and shouting: 12-year-old Sam Burrows's habit of spending twenty-five minutes each morning deciding what to wear. Even though Ira knew Sam's early-morning sartorial finickiness was a sign of school anxiety, it still drove him crazy. But he finally found a solution to it in Sam's love of rock 'n' roll. With the help of a music encyclopedia bought at a secondhand book store, Ira created the Ira Burrows Daily Rock 'n' Roll quiz. Consisting of ten questions, it is administered each morning during dressing time, and has proven to be such a big success that Sam's dressing time has been cut by three-quarters. So too has the incidence of father-son shouting matches in the Burrows household.

*Redirect problematic impulses.* These impulses also contribute to many provocative misbehaviors. In the case of a Type A boy or girl, the most problematic impulses are aggressiveness, leadership, and competitiveness. Lacking other outlets for his forcefulness, the Type A hits his little brother; the outlet for his desire to lead is to bully him; and the outlet for his competitiveness is to constantly remind his little brother how much smarter, faster, and better-looking he is.

Redirecting problematic impulses is based on the premise that finding a more constructive outlet for a troublesome impulse almost always will lessen the misbehavior it produces. A good example of how the strategy works is the way Bill Nolan used it to solve a discipline problem that had produced more than father-son shouting matches in the Nolan home. On two occasions, it led Bill to strike 12-year-old Louis Nolan. Bill's behavior may make him sound like a harsh parent, and certainly that's the picture of the authoritarian discipliner painted by Dr. Bracke's data. But in Type A homes, such a figure is much more likely to be, as Bill is, a very provoked, beleaguered, put-upon parent.

A great many of his disciplinary problems with Louis can be explained by the fact that Louis is the Type A child I described above, 8-year-old Willy Nolan, the little brother; and Bill the kind of parent who gets upset watching one of his children torment the other on a daily—sometimes hourly—basis.

It says something about Bill Nolan's conscientiousness as a parent that a few days after the second hitting incident, he was in my office asking for help. He had already made the discovery that authoritarian discipliners usually take a long time to make: that in the end, hitting, shouting, and threatening increase rather than decrease the incidence of disciplinary problems. In the Nolan home, this truism had produced a predictable pattern. Coming down hard on Louis would win Willy a few days of peace, but once the torment resumed—and it always did—it did so with renewed vigor and intensity.

I told Bill that there was a simple reason for the spiraling violence. The humiliation of being hit, threatened, and yelled at makes a child so angry that it inspires revenge fantasies. But since a 100-pound child can't act out his fantasies against the 180-pound adult who inspires them, he targets his 70-pound younger brother. I also told Bill that there were more constructive ways of dealing with Louis's disciplinary infractions. For the next hour or so, I described most of the strategies in this chapter, but I put a special emphasis on rechanneling problematic impulses because I felt Willy's torment wouldn't come to a permanent end until the impulses driving his tormentor found a healthier expression.

In the case of aggressiveness and competitiveness, the best place to find a healthy outlet is outside the home in physical activities such as baseball, basketball, and soccer. The A's leadership impulses, however, can often be satisfied directly within the context of the big brother–little brother relationship. There are a lot of things 12-year-olds know that 8-year-olds do not. During our conversation, I told Bill that encouraging Louis to share his knowledge with Willy not only would satisfy his leaderly impulses and give him a reason to feel good about himself, but it would teach Willy some things he needed to know.

To some degree, what a big brother teaches a little brother depends on big brother's skill and little brother's interests. I knew, for example, that the Nolan boys shared an interest in Indian artifacts, so I suggested that Louis might show Willy how to carve an arrowhead. I also knew that both boys were baseball fans, so I recommended that Louis be encouraged to share some of his hitting and fielding secrets with Willy.

In addition, there are some more general skills that every big brother can pass on to a younger sibling. In the Nolan household, these included Louis's special knowledge of how to talk to girls, dress for a dance, and buy Mom and Dad birthday and anniversary gifts. As I suspected, passing them on to Willy has made Louis feel so big and powerful and smart that the tormenting behavior Bill Nolan found so provocative has ended.

*Be a thoughtful limit-setter.* This is a third way to prevent provocative misbehaviors, and it involves something more than the usual limit-setting mothers and fathers do. There are certain situations so fraught with temptation that they can increase drastically the normal propensity to misbehave. One case is the child's first unsupervised visit to an evening movie with friends; another is the big party your 15-year-old desperately wants to attend, even though you know the host's parents will be in Bermuda the night of the party.

Thoughtful limit-setting involves identifying these disciplinary hot spots beforehand and imposing firm, clear guidelines to govern behavior in them. In the first case, the parent should state very explicitly that because bad things can happen to children who are out by themselves at night, at pickup time, the child and his friends should be standing in front of the theater, and not wandering around the adjacent mall. In the case of the 15-year-old, explain that because regrettable things can happen at unsupervised teenage parties, for this party you are lowering his normal weekend curfew from 11:00 P.M. to 10:00 P.M.

Since no technique is foolproof, the preventive measures I've just outlined won't always be enough to keep a Type A out of harm's way. Bored by shopping chores, she may suddenly revert to her old disruptive self, or annoyed at younger brother Willy, he may suddenly revert to his old bullying self. Preventive discipline's last two techniques are designed to help a parent deal with these borderline situations.

The first is a *statement of parental expectations about appropriate behavior.* Telling the youngster, "In this family, people are expected to respect one another," or, "In this supermarket, customers are expected to behave themselves," acts like a two-minute warning. It tells the A clearly that he is nearing the border of misbehavior. But because the warning comes in the form of a parental expectation, it avoids the accusatory—and hence self-esteem–damaging—tone of a warning, which focuses directly on the child, as in: "If you do that again, you're going to be in big trouble."

If the situation continues to escalate, a *choice* should be offered. A statement like, "No running in the supermarket. You can either walk or sit in the cart where I can keep an eye on you," reminds the child of what she's probably forgotten in the heat of the moment: that misbehaviors often have unhappy consequences. But because such statements leave the child a choice about what to do next, they also preserve self-esteem.

*Make reprimands self-esteem positive.* If the child chooses to step over the line, how can a parent express her displeasure and unhappiness and still prevent her child from feeling humiliated and belittled?

One way is by imposing a cooling off period on herself. It's very hard to focus on the self-esteem needs of a child who has just broken a favorite vase or given his little sister a black eye. So, if the Type A does something truly upsetting, don't reprimand him immediately. Instead, tell him you are too angry to discuss his disciplinary infraction now and instruct him to go to his room; you'll join him for a conversation once you have calmed down.

Another way to keep reprimands positive is by remembering that criticizing the misbehavior and not the child is as much a part of good parental discipline as it is good parental communication.

A third way is to employ strategy I mentioned in chapter 9: acknowledge the legitimate feelings of the perpetrator. Not every disciplinary infraction falls into this category, but a surprisingly large number of misbehaviors do spring from justifiable anger, impatience, frustration, or anxiety. Diedre Falk is once again a case in point.

A supermarket isn't a very stimulating environment for a 6-year-old, so Diedre has a perfect right to be bored. An admonition like, "I know shopping isn't fun for you, but that doesn't give you the right to turn the supermarket aisles into a race track," is a way of saluting Diedre's legitimate feeling, while also letting her know how much parental displeasure her disruptive behavior is causing.

#### SKILL TWO: LOGICAL AND NATURAL CONSEQUENCES

If you look at children who possess a firm sense of right and wrong, you'll find that they not only like and respect themselves, they also possess the ability to reason morally. This is the second building block of moral acuity, and in its most fundamental sense it means the capacity to think through the consequences of an action before taking it. A Bobby O'Donnell who could do this might still have been annoyed at finding a seat he coveted occupied, but knowing that his bullying would humiliate the seat's occupier and land him in the principal's office, Bobby would have known that bullying wasn't the right way to handle the problem.

How can a disciplining parent foster such moral reasoning in her Type A?

One way is by taking the time to explain to him why a misdeed is wrong. The harmful or dangerous consequences of an infraction may be evident to you, but sometimes they won't be to the child who has committed it.

Another way is by imposing penalties that are logical enough to enhance the child's understanding of why an action produces a dangerous or harmful consequence, tailored enough to help him understand the degree of wrongdoing it involves, and fair enough to avoid the anger and hostility that can impair his ability to contemplate the first two points.

Logical and natural consequences, the two disciplining techniques that make up Skill Two of respect-oriented discipline, meet all these criteria, and since natural consequences is the simpler of the two procedures, let's begin with it.

Every behavior has a consequence. Stand out in the rain and you get wet, stay up late and the next morning you are tired. Natural consequences is based on the premise that the consequences of many misbehaviors are sufficiently logical and unpleasant to provide their own self-explanatory punishments. Take the teenager who spends his allowance by Wednesday. The natural consequence of such an act is a logical and self-evident penalty—you spend the next four days broke. Or take the child who ignores his room chores. The natural consequences of that infraction also is a logical, self-evident penalty—you live in a messy room.

Another of the governing premises of natural consequences is that by largely removing the parent from the disciplinary process, a major distraction is eliminated. With no one to get angry at or blame, full attention can be given to contemplating the misbehavior and its consequences. Generally, the child who has been given such an opportunity will think twice before committing the misbehavior again. Roberta Ward is a case in point.

On the night of an important date, Roberta was horrified to see a favorite black sweater lying wrinkled and unwashed on the bookshelf where she had tossed it two days earlier. Furious, Roberta was about to blow up at her mother, when she remembered Susan Ward's hamper edict: only clothes deposited in the laundry hamper get washed. This incident hasn't transformed Roberta into a moral philosopher, but Susan reports that ever since, Roberta has been almost religious in her observation of the hamper edict.

A third ruling principle of natural consequences is that it requires a stout parental heart. A beseeching child should always be provided with an explanation: "We agreed your allowance was for seven days, not three," or, "You promised to pick up your room." But that's all. Caving in and providing the loan or room service the beseecher wants will obscure the point of the exercise, which is to teach him that unpleasant actions lead to unpleasant consequences.

One caveat about natural consequences: there are a few situations when it ceases to be an appropriate teaching tool. The first is when the consequences of a misbehavior are too pleasant or obscure to teach a child that unhappy behaviors produce unhappy consequences. An example of such a misbehavior would be violating a parental injunction against eating junk food. A second instance is when the consequences of a misdeed are too dangerous to be experienced. No parent would want her 5-year-old experiencing the natural consequences of ignoring a ban on crossing the street by himself. The third situation is when the consequences of a misdeed endanger or disrupt others.

In these situations, the appropriate disciplinary technique is logical consequences. It too is designed to promote moral reasoning, but since it deals with a different class of misdeeds, it employs different teaching tools.

One of the most important is parental explanation. Because the results of a disciplinary infraction are either too obscure or unpleasant, or dangerous, the parent steps in and makes the necessary logical connections for the child. In the case of a 6-, or 7-year-old who violates a parental rule about twice-daily tooth brushing, an example of the technique would be to point out what won't be obvious to the perpetrator: that violating this rule allows bacteria to build up in the teeth, and the natural consequences of bacteria buildup are cavities and toothaches.

In some cases, the parent doesn't have to be quite so explicit.

Take the 5-year-old who ignores the rule about crossing the street by himself. Asking him, "What if a car suddenly appeared?" encourages him to think about the logical consequence of his misdeed. Or take the 10-year-old who decides to wander around the mall, despite being told to wait in front of the movie theater. Asking him what would happen if a dangerous stranger appeared during his wanderings is a way of getting him to think about a possible consequence of his misdeed.

In logical consequences, a parent also plays a much more active part in drafting penalties and punishments. These too should help enhance the child's ability to identify the consequences of his actions. That is what a penalty does when it is shaped according to the following four rules.

The first is that *it should be logically related to the infraction that inspired it*. One example of such a penalty is requiring the child who makes a mess in the living room to clean up the mess. Another is requiring the teenager who goes $100 over budget on a prom outfit to work off the $100 in chores. Because both penalties flow naturally out of the children's misdeeds, they enhance the perpetrators' ability to identify the consequences of their actions in a way that, say, suspending the TV privileges of the messy child, and grounding the overspending child, wouldn't.

A second rule of punishment is that *it should always be tailored to the degree of wrongdoing involved in a misbehavior*. You and I know that stealing produces more serious consequences than going $100 over budget on a prom outfit, but a child won't be entirely clear about this important distinction unless the first behavior is penalized more severely than the second.

A third rule of punishment is that *the misbehaving child should be asked what he thinks would be an appropriate penalty for his wrongdoing*. I know that some parents will have reservations about this rule. But besides encouraging the Type A to think hard about the degree of his wrongdoing and its consequences, such a question also is a mark of respect. It says, "I think you are mature and fair-minded enough not only to realize you have done something wrong, but to want to make amends for it."

The last rule of punishment is to *avoid harshness*. Upon occasion, a raised voice is appropriate, but no matter how serious the infraction, a parent should never shout, threaten, or hit. Besides producing needless humiliation and belittlement, these practices will produce such anger and hostility in the child that he won't have the clarity of mind or the desire to contemplate the consequences of his wrongdoing.

Although I suspect most readers are aware of it, I should point out that both natural and logical consequences have one major drawback. In time, energy, patience, and in the ability to keep one's temper in check, they demand far more from a parent than does authoritarian discipline. Once a Type A learns the lessons they teach, however, a parent no longer has to worry about how the child will react when a classmate takes a coveted seat or he's losing a game he dearly wants to win.

Equally important, she will also no longer have to worry how her A will respond if another youngster asks, "Do you want a drink?" or, "Do you want to do some coke?" A principal reason youngsters say "yes" to such propositions is that they lack the ability to see down what road the "yes" will take them—or, to put it in the terms of this chapter, they lack the ability to reason morally.

### GIVE THE TYPE A MORE OF WHAT HE WANTS: YOU

In many ways, 11-year-old Peter Le Cinq exemplifies all the qualities that make a positive Type A such an exemplary child. Peter is a good student, a natural leader, and, in almost every conceivable situation, energetic, forceful, and engaging. But Peter's otherwise exemplary self is marred by one failing: Whenever he steps into public with either of his parents, he has a habit of waiting until the largest number of people are within earshot, then whispering in the loudest possible stage whisper, "Oh, fuck."

Charles and Marie Le Cinq know enough about their son in particular, and child psychology in general, to know what's going on. Peter's public use of foul language is a form of that oldest of childhood pastimes, parent baiting; but what baffles the Le Cinqs, who are in many ways as exemplary as their son, is why Peter feels the need to bait them.

The answer is simple. He desperately wants their attention—which is to say, he desperately wants more of them.

While all misbehaviors have an element of attention-getting in them, the incidence of disciplinary infractions, which are motivated primarily by this desire, has increased dramatically over the past decade. You don't have to look any further than friends, neighbors, or yourself to understand why. With dual-career couples now the rule rather than the exception, time has become a very precious commodity in most families. When parents aren't busy with work, they are busy with household chores, and often the upshot is that the child feels so neglected, he begins swearing or engaging in other disciplinary infractions to catch the eye of his busy parents.

Self-esteem-positive reprimands, a preventive-discipline mentality, natural and logical consequences—all the disciplinary techniques I have described can help control this problem, but they won't solve it because they don't give the youngster what he wants.

What can solve it is knowing how to make the most of your shared time. There are several ways to do this. One is to regularize it by setting aside specific, agreed-upon moments when parent and Type A child do nothing but be with each other. This could be a half-hour after school, or an hour in the evening before bed, or several hours on the weekend. What matters more than when the time is spent is that it is inviolate. The youngster should know that, short of an emergency, this is a period he can always plan on spending with Mom or Dad.

Also important is that the time be left unstructured. I realize that for parents who are themselves Type A's, this won't be easy. But it is during unstructured time that the parent-child relationship acquires a place in the child's memory and feelings and this produces its special ability to comfort and nurture a lonely boy or girl.

For instance, even on his bluest days, 10-year-old Billy Davis finds himself smiling when he thinks about a conversation he and his father, Wally, had during such a shared time. Its subject was Batman, or more specifically, the color of Batman's outfit. Puzzled at why it was black in the movie but always blue in the comic books, Billy asked his father what the reason for this difference was.

"Oh, simple," Wally Davis replied. "In the comic book, Batman always wears his away uniform."

Moments like this can't be manufactured or forced; they just have to happen. But one way to help them happen is to make sure that during shared time, parent and child describe the high and low points of their respective days. Often the stories that emerge from these exchanges will, like Billy's Batman story, keep the parent such a fresh and palpable presence in the child's mind that he won't feel the need to engage in attention-getting behaviors.

# 11

# Changing the Type A's Values

Imagine a pyramid turned upside down, with the words *aggression, exhibition, dominance, autonomy,* and *accumulation* written on top, and *achievement* and *winning* at the base, and you'll have a good idea of how the Type A child's value system looks. The pyramid takes the shape it does because of the depth of the A's insecurities.

The desire to win and achieve, which begins as a way of assuaging this insecurity, becomes something else over time. "I want and need to win and achieve" becomes "I value winning and achievement." Then, over time, "I value winning and achievement" becomes "I value outshining (exhibition), owning more than others (accumulation), getting my own way (dominance), and elbowing aside the competition (aggression)."

Consider the threat these values pose to your Type A's happiness and heart, and you'll understand the importance this chapter places on value change. In one sense, you may already be fostering good values. Qualities such as altruism, cooperation, empathy, and nurturance flow naturally from a strong, secure sense of self, just as values such as aggression and dominance flow from a weak, self-doubting ego. So, if you're pres-

**168**

ently employing the self-esteem-boosting strategies described in the last three chapters, you're already changing your Type A's beliefs.

In this chapter, you will learn two ways to hasten the pace of change. One is called values clarification and is directed at your child; the other involves role modeling and is directed at you.

Do you remember the angry preschool Type A's who leaped up and punched the Bobo doll when they lost a toy-car race? When I introduced those youngsters in chapter 1, I pointed out that one reason for their furious reaction was damaged self-esteem. Defeat had made their fragile egos go "ouch." But there also was another reason—parental role modeling—and Dr. Tiffany Field touched on its influence in her report on the toddlers. Very likely, she said, they come from homes where parents behave as if winning is all. Therefore, when these youngsters lose, they act as if they've lost all.

Like Dr. Field, most other experts believe that you can't talk about the nature of the Type A child's value system without talking about his parental role models. Loving Mom and Dad, the child wants to be like them. Thus, when Mom and Dad behave in ways that endorse values such as achievement, accumulation, and dominance, it reinforces the Type A's own predisposition toward these values.

I can already see self-accusing fingers beginning to rise. Please put them down. You can't come of age in our society without absorbing at least a few Type A values. The object of the exercise below is to help you identify the ones that may be making you an unconscious contributor to your Type A's value pyramid.

## VALUES ASSESSMENT TRAINING

Developed with the assistance of Dr. Kevin Kelly of Purdue University, and incorporating several of his research techniques, VAT allows you to pinpoint your hidden Type A values through a technique called "value recordkeeping." How we spend our time says a great deal about what we value. Thus, by keeping a record of your activities over a specific period, you can get a pretty good idea of the values you prize most.

What makes such information an important agent in reconstructing your Type A's value pyramid is your parental love. No matter what their predilections, youngsters rarely espouse values their parents don't, and since it is rare that parents consciously model values they know to be harmful, often just knowing what your hidden Type A values are will produce the kind of behavioral change in you that will lead to a value change in your Type A.

Here's how VAT works:

Begin by reading through the list of values below and choosing the five that you believe best describe you.

*Achievement.* Aspires to accomplish difficult tasks. Maintains high standards and is willing to work toward distant goals. Responds positively to competition. Willing to make all-out effort to attain excellence.

*Accumulation.* Desires to gain possessions and property, to work very hard for money and goods. Derives pleasure in owning more than others.

*Aggression.* Enjoys combat and argument and is easily annoyed. Sometimes willing to hurt people to get own way. May seek to get even with those whom he believes have harmed him.

*Autonomy.* Breaks away from restraints or restrictions of any kind. Desires to have own way. Enjoys being free and unattached to others.

*Dominance.* Attempts to control environment and to direct and dominate other people. Expresses opinions forcefully. Enjoys the role of leader and may assume it spontaneously.

*Endurance.* Willing to work long hours. Doesn't give up quickly on a problem. Perseveres even in the face of great difficulty. Persistent and unrelenting in work habits.

*Exhibition.* Wants to be the center of attention, enjoys having an audience. Engages in behavior that wins the attention of others.

*Nurturance.* Gives sympathy or comfort, assists others whenever possible. Interested in caring for the less fortunate. Offers a helping hand to those in need. Readily performs favors for others.

*Cooperation.* Enjoys working with others, and puts a high value on ability to get along with them.

*Friendship.* Enjoys having a large circle of acquaintances and draws sustenance in being with them.

*Compassion.* Worries about the well-being of others. Devotes time and money to the poor and disadvantaged.

*Play-relaxation.* Does things just for the fun of it. Spends a good deal of time participating in games, sports, and social activities. Enjoys jokes and funny stories, tries to maintain a light, easygoing attitude.

*Empathy.* Believes it's important to understand the thoughts and feelings of others and to respect them in all situations.

*Recognition.* Desires to be held in high esteem by others. Concerned with reputation and with what other people think. Works for the approval and recognition of others.

I believe the five values that best describe me are:

1. _____
2. _____
3. _____
4. _____
5. _____

How much time did you devote last week to each of the following activities? (Weekly participation in community and social organizations, which don't fall within the three-day re-cordkeeping period, also should be included.)

Work (include only hours worked above normal work week) _____

Participation in social and community organizations _____

Studying or other forms of self-improvement _____

Charitable work _____

Playing with child _____

Relaxing with spouse _____

Watching TV/reading _____

Pursuing hobbies and other leisure-time activities _____

Housework _____

Shopping _____

Talking to friends _____

Arranging records and files _____

Counseling friend, child, or spouse _____

Preparing yourself for career advancement (e.g., attending seminars, taking classes) _____

Guiding and directing others (at home, at work, or
during leisure-time activities)                                    _____
Debating or arguing with friends, family, or colleagues  _____
Organizing activities and chores for others              _____
Working at or attending church or temple                 _____
Other (specify) _____         _____

In order, list the five activities you spent the most time on:
1. _____
2. _____
3. _____
4. _____
5. _____

In order, list the values these activities reflect (e.g., a high
score on shopping could reflect a high priority on accumulation
or exhibitionism; a high score on arguing and debating, a high
priority on aggression or achievement; a high score on organizing activities for others, a high priority on dominance; etc.)
1. _____
2. _____
3. _____
4. _____
5. _____

Now, go back and examine the list of values you said best
described you. Values that appear on the above list, but not on
your original list, are your hidden values (i.e., values you are
unconsciously expressing in your behavior). If among them are
achievement, accumulation, autonomy, dominance, endurance,
exhibition, and recognition, write them on the list below.
My hidden Type A values are:
1. _____
2. _____
3. _____
4. _____
5. _____

When I'm administering VAT to a parent, usually two questions arise. The first concerns the parent herself. "Now that I

know what my hidden Type A values are," she'll say, "how can I stop modeling them?"

In my experience, often the self-awareness that VAT produces is enough to modify such modeling. As I pointed out earlier, frequently, merely knowing your Type A values is its own deterrent. Since these values are continually being reinforced by the culture, however, you may wish an additional antidote. I would recommended two books: *Treating Type A Behavior and Your Heart,* by Dr. Meyer Friedman and Diane Ulmer, RN, and *Stress Management for the Healthy Type A,* by Dr. Ethel Roskies. Both contain excellent strategies for the adult Type A who wishes to effect value change in himself.

Parents whose hidden Type A values include potentially beneficial values such as achievement, autonomy, endurance, and domination (which is usually listed as leadership) often ask, "How can I show my child the best side of these values?"

Here are some ways parental role modeling can be used to answer this question.

*Achievement.* To make this value work for him, a Type A needs to know three things about achievement. The first is that other things matter, too. You can use your modeling to make this point by showing him how much time you make in your life for him, for your family, for your friends, and for your hobbies and avocations. Spending a Sunday afternoon with a book or a Saturday morning in an aerobics class not only benefits you, but it teaches your child a valuable lesson about priorities.

The second thing a youngster needs to know about achievement is that, contrary to the Type A philosophy, it doesn't always have to involve beating the competition; you can also achieve by satisfying yourself. And that is the message conveyed by a parent who takes palpable satisfaction in bringing a garden to life, or preparing a gourmet meal, or painting a picture, or helping a friend.

Finally, a child needs to learn that an occasional failure to achieve is not the end of the world. Modeling this point can be difficult. Not getting a hoped-for-promotion or job hurts. But conducting yourself with calm and dignity in moments of defeat teaches the Type A a lesson about achievement he'll still be benefiting from at 30 or 40.

*Autonomy.* While this value also can be beneficial, the child who cherishes independence too highly will resist establishing himself in the social community and in school affiliations, which can give his life meaning and lower his risk of heart disease.

So, how do you persuade your Type A to surrender a little of his precious autonomy?

Demonstrating the pleasure you derive from working with others is one way. Even the most autonomous-minded child is likely to rethink his allegiance to independence if he lives in a home where being a PTA officer or serving on a church or community board is a palpable source of parental pride. Describing how supportive and helpful people are to you is another way. Just ask Lynn Davis. Mentioning how helpful her friends and colleagues are, produced a discernible change in her 10-year-old son, Billy. These days Billy spends fewer afternoons alone in his room and more at the park. A few weeks ago, to Lynn's delight, Billy joined his school's glee club.

I won't say that Billy is now going to grow into one of my most gregarious and outstanding kids, but he is likely to become more receptive to people because his mother's role modeling has taught him that people can be trusted. And for the Type A who learns that, autonomy and independence don't seem quite so important anymore.

*Domination/leadership.* Overseeing an office of thirty attorneys has taught Mike Denko that one characteristic of a good leader is to let others lead at times. Recently, Mike used his role modeling to pass this important lesson on to his son, 11-year-old Jeffrey. On hearing that Mike had volunteered for the assistant manager's job on his Little League team, Jeff reacted with disbelief and profound mortification. What would the other kids think when they learned that his father was only a lowly assistant manager? Moreover, Jeffrey was not shy about sharing this concern with his father. But once the season began, he experienced a change of heart. Seeing how much satisfaction his dad got out of his job and how much respect he received from the rest of the team, Jeffrey not only felt proud, rather than embarrassed by Mike.

*Endurance.* One of the things a child needs to learn to benefit from this value is that too much endurance can be counterproductive. A good example of how role modeling can make this point is the strategy the mother of one of my A's used when her marathon effort to produce a new set of budget figures produced a record number of mistakes. The day after being told about the errors by her department superior, the mother mentioned the incident to her daughter at breakfast and added, "You know why I got the figures wrong? I tried to do too much. I make my worst mistakes when I'm overtired. If I'd waited and finished up the next morning when I was fresh, I wouldn't have made so many silly errors."

Another thing a child needs to learn about endurance is that sometimes you have to give yourself permission *not* to endure. The parent who gives herself permission to take a weekly aerobics class or go out to lunch with a friend is using her modeling to make this point.

## VALUES CLARIFICATION

Inside every child is another person. Some call him the youngster's conscience, others his better self, still others his guardian angel. But whatever name he goes by, this figure always displays the same characteristics: he speaks in a powerful voice. If he says "don't," usually the child won't. Values clarification helps enlist this influential figure as an ally in promoting value change.

Values clarification is based on a technique we looked at in the last chapter: moral reasoning. Values produce consequences, and as values clarification brings the child to the realization that a common consequence of many Type A values is selfish, hurtful, or self-punishing behavior, you can count on the inner voice to nudge him toward value change.

The following techniques are adapted from the strategies Sidney Simon developed in his book *Values Clarification: Practical Strategies for Teachers.*

1. *Help your child define his Type A values.*
The questions below are designed to help your youngster (and you) identify the priority he attaches to autonomy, achievement, dominance, cooperation, work, friendship, and other values that have a direct bearing on Type A behavior. After he's

completed the questions, jointly review the answers and, based on his replies, draw up a list of his top five values.

### a.  What would you prefer to do?

Improve your math                                              _____
Make a new friend                                              _____
Get a new bike for your birthday                               _____

### b.  What would you do if a classmate said something mean to you?

Hit him                                                        _____
Complain to the teacher                                        _____
Ignore his remark                                              _____

### c.  What would you consider worse?

Telling on a friend                                            _____
Failing a test                                                 _____

### d.  What do you dislike most about your brother and/or sister?

He/she tells you what to do                                    _____
He/she ignores you                                             _____
He/she never listens to your problems                          _____

### e.  What would you most want in a friend?

Someone who will agree with you                                _____
Someone who is aware of other people's needs                   _____

### f.  If you had a problem, what would you do?

Ask a friend for help                                          _____
Ask a parent for help                                          _____
Try to solve it yourself                                       _____

### g.  If you had $20, how would you spend it?

Shopping                                                       _____
Entertainment                                                  _____

**h. Which do you like to play most?**

Team sports like baseball and football _____
Personal sports like tennis and swimming _____

**i. What quality best describes the job you'd like to have when you grow up?**

It allows you to help others _____
It makes you rich _____
It gives you a chance to make an important
scientific discovery _____

**j. What would you most like to improve?**

Your looks _____
The way you use time _____
Your social life _____

**k. When do you have the most fun?**

When you are alone _____
With a large group _____
With a few friends _____

**l. What do you prefer?**

Organizing activities for friends _____
Letting someone else do the organizing _____
Jointly deciding with friends what games to
play _____

**m. What is the most important quality in a friend?**

Loyalty _____
Generosity _____
Honesty _____

**n. What would be hardest for you?**

To admit you told a lie _____
To tell someone you broke a window _____
To admit you cheated _____

o. **Which subjects do you like most?**

Math _____
Social studies _____
English _____

p. **What would you most like to do?**

Listen to music _____
Watch a play _____
Listen to a debate _____

q. **What would you find hardest?**

Show your parents a poor grade _____
Walk away from an argument or disagreement _____
Take direction from another child _____

The choices these questions require a child to make should provide a pretty clear picture of his values. But to give you some examples, a child who finds it hard to show a parent a poor grade, or prefers to improve his math scores over the other choices, puts a high value on achievement. The youngster who finds it hard to walk away from an argument, likes listening to debates, and would hit a rude classmate ranks highly on aggression. Similarly, a child who prefers to solve his own problems, likes personal sports such as tennis and swimming, and has the most fun when he's alone, puts a high value on autonomy. Domination is a high priority for the youngster who wants a friend who agrees with him and finds it hard to take direction from peers. Even a youngster's favorite school subjects say a lot about his value system. Generally, boys and girls who like math also prize autonomy, while those who prefer English and history put a higher premium on social values.

My child's top values are:
1. _____
2. _____
3. _____

4. _____
5. _____


2. *Show your child the consequences of his values.*

Have your youngster read through the situations described
below and then ask him how he would respond to each, given
his values. (For example, given his attachment to achievement,
how would he respond to your suggestion that he put aside his
studies for the evening and join you for a movie?) Make sure his
answers are logical. That is, make sure they are true to the
values revealed in step 1; otherwise, he may miss the point of
this exercise, which is to demonstrate that selfish, hurtful, and
self-punishing behavior is a logical consequence of many Type A
values (when taken to the extremes Type A's take them to).

Your friend asks if you'll tutor him the night before a big
math test. But you want to see a movie.
    How would you respond? _____
_____

You want to be in the school play, but you're only offered a
minor part, not the lead.
    How would you respond? _____
_____

Another child inadvertently says something that angers you.
You know he didn't mean it, and if you were alone, you'd ignore
it, but all your friends are present.
    How would you respond? _____
_____

You're in danger of losing a race for class president. A friend
offers a suggestion: Why don't you try to undermine your opponent by circulating unflattering rumors about him?
    How would you respond? _____
_____

You're asked to work with a group of underprivileged youngsters in your community. You know you can help them, but you
also know that will leave you with less time for yourself.
    How would you respond? _____
_____

A classmate who has forgotten his lunch money asks to borrow five dollars. You have it, but plan to go shopping after school.

How would you respond? _____

_____

You're asked to step aside and let another child lead the class. How would you respond? _____

_____


3. *Conduct an alternative-value search.*

For a youngster who puts a high priority on Type A values, many of step 2's revelations will be painful. For example, if accumulation is a high priority, he'll find that acting in accord with it requires him to say no to the friend who wants to borrow lunch money (otherwise, he'll have to forgo shopping at the mall), and if he prizes achievement, he'll probably say no to the underprivileged children who need his help. (How can he take away from the studies he needs to achieve?)

Step 3 is designed to introduce the child to values that have logical consequences which will be more acceptable to his better self. Here's how it works.

Begin by picking one of the situations in step 2 (or, if you'd prefer, a real life one your Type A has been recently involved in), then ask him to write down three ways of responding to it. Say, for example, the situation you choose is the classmate who has inadvertently said something insulting. Your A's three responses to it might be: Hit the classmate; let the remark pass; or warn the classmate what will happen if he repeats his mistake.

Next, jointly figure out the logical consequences of each choice and the value it reflects. In this case, such an exercise would produce the following result.

Choice 1: Hit the classmate
Consequence: Physical injury/humiliation
Value: Domination/aggression
Choice 2: Ignore the remark
Consequence: Gratitude and esteem of classmate

Value: Empathy, or the ability to understand how another
    feels.
Choice 3: Warn the classmate
Consequence: Humiliation and fear
Value: Domination

By the fifth or sixth time you use this technique, your Type A
will see a pattern. Certain values, like empathy, altruism, and
nurturance, produce the right behaviors in every situation,
while other values like dominance, aggression, and autonomy
(when taken to extremes) produce the wrong behaviors. Once
this pattern is clear, usually your Type A's conscience will take
over and do the rest of the work.

### OTHER WAYS TO PROMOTE VALUE CHANGE

It's 10:30 on a brisk Saturday morning, and I'm sitting in a
classroom at my local high school with a group of 14-, 15-, and
16-year-olds who are here for a peer-counseling session. Peer
counseling involves kids helping kids, and I'm at this particular
session as a kind of visiting dignitary. Two years ago, my wife
and I were part of the parents' group that organized the peer-
counseling program for our local high school, and as a way of
saying thanks, occasionally the administration invites me to sit
in on sessions.

Unofficially, I'm here to observe a patient who serves as a
counselor in the program. She's Peggy Duckworth, a tall blond
girl with braided hair who blushed when I walked in. (Can you
imagine anything more mortifying than meeting your pediatrician in a public place!) I've known Peggy for several years, but
once the session begins, I see a new side of her. Advising Tommy
Fitzgerald, one of the "troubled" children who are in the group
for counseling, Peggy is sensitive, thoughtful, even wise. Listening, I permit myself a small smile of satisfaction. The self-
centered teenager I used to know has blossomed into a compas-
sionate young woman.

Six months ago, when I recommended the peer-counseling
program to Peggy's parents, I couldn't have guaranteed such a
transformation. But experience has taught me that community-

and school-based programs like this are an excellent vehicle for promoting value change in youngsters like Peggy. They tend to push the self-absorbed A out of himself and introduce him to the joys and satisfaction of working with and helping others.

For young children, the activities most likely to promote this discovery and social values like cooperation, altruism, and empathy include scouting, Little League, and volunteer work at a church or synagogue. For teens, the options are much wider. In addition to peer counseling, there are Big Brother and Big Sister programs, which pair up older adolescents with children who need role models. Many hospitals, nursing homes, and daycare centers run volunteer programs that give the teens an opportunity to experience the rewards of helping those who truly need help.

Some junior high schools also run what are known as community outreach programs. These are designed to enliven and dramatize civics classes by getting students actively involved in community issues. For example, one group of students in my town recently assisted some senior citizens who were having trouble getting heat in their homes, while another got involved in a drive to clean up the town's parks. If your Type A's school offers such an outreach program, encourage him to join. Community involvement is not only a good vehicle for value change, it's also good training for tomorrow's leaders.

Family activities are another good way to foster the Type A's allegiance to social values. Like all youngsters, the lessons the A learns at home are the ones that have the deepest influence on him. Discovering at dinner that mom can help him solve a problem, or that he can help big sister solve one, teaches him about the joys and rewards of social interaction not only within the family but of social interactions generally. And a Type A learns this lesson quickest in a home that follows these rules:

• Have dinner together at least four nights a week.
• Turn child-centered activities, like visits to the zoo and circus, into family-centered activities by including both parents.
• Reserve at least one weekend a month for a family activity like a picnic or camping trip.

One last point before we leave values: Don't be afraid to talk over your beliefs with your child. A lot of parents shy away from such conversations, largely, I suspect, because they are afraid of sounding like *their* parents, who couldn't talk about values without standing on a soap box. However, children need parental instruction on the big issues, and if you listen as well as advise during values conversations, you can offer such instruction without sounding pompous or preachy.

# 12

# Teaching the Type A Child How to Manage His High-Strung Temperament

No matter how else your Type A changes, one thing won't change. Waiting in line at the movie theater, he'll still be the first child in his group to become impatient, and on the morning of the big test or the night of the big party, he'll still be more prone to anxiety than are his friends.

This lingering vulnerability to stress highlights a major limitation of the strategies I've described in the last five chapters. At best, the high self-esteem these strategies promote provides only a partial antidote to the A's high-strung temperament. The techniques that make up this chapter are designed to provide the remainder.

Taken together, they allow the Type A to manage his volatile temperament in a way which ensures that, even if the party becomes very anxiety-provoking or the wait at the movie theater very frustrating, he won't lose control and do or say something that creates a problem for himself or others.

What are the techniques?

The first is: *Teach the Type A to identify the signs of stress.*

Before a child can learn how to counter stress, he has to learn how to tell when he's feeling stressed. He needs to be aware of the most common physical and emotional symptoms of stress and he also needs to know which situations and events are most likely to trigger these symptoms in him. The two lists below are designed to help you foster such knowledge in your Type A.

As you go over the first list with your A, ask him if he recalls experiencing any of the symptoms, and how often; as you go over the second, ask him which situations and events most often produce these symptoms in him.

*Physical and Emotional Symptoms of Stress*

Stomach problems, including diarrhea, constipation, nausea, and heartburn
Rapid heartbeat
Ache in the neck, lower back, or jaw
Muscle jerks or tics
Eating problems—constant eating, loss of appetite
Sleeping problems—unable to fall asleep, waking up in the middle of the night
Chronic fatigue
Restlessness
Teeth grinding
Dry throat or mouth
Shortness of breath
General anxiety, nervous feeling, or tenseness
Dizziness or weakness
Irritability
Depression
Accident prone
Feeling overwhelmed and unable to cope
Chronic boredom
Inability to discuss problems with others
Fear of heights or closed spaces
Feeling rejected
Inability to concentrate or finish projects
Always in a hurry

*Situations Most Commonly Associated with the Production of
Stress Symptoms in a Type A*

Trying out for school event or athletic team
Asked to wait
Hand not acknowledged by teacher
Criticism
When someone says something challenging or provocative
Need to make a decision
Going on a date
Visiting a separated or divorced parent
Meeting parent's new boy- or girlfriend
Parent drinks too much
Falling behind schedule
When the house becomes noisy
Lacks money to do things child wants
No one to play with
Watching certain TV programs and movies or listening to
    certain music (find out which ones)
In the presence of certain peers (find out which ones)
Embarrassed
Lacks time to play
When child thinks about the way he looks
Pressured to do something he doesn't want to do
Denied privileges that friends have—like right to watch cer-
    tain movies or late curfew hour
In the presence of certain teachers (find out which ones)
When sick
Leaving home for school
When praised
When he thinks how long it takes to grow up
When child feels he hasn't accomplished enough

### STRESS MANAGEMENT

Once you and your Type A have identified his high-stress
situations, how can you together help him manage them in a
way that lowers their emotional temperature?

For some situations, one good strategy is avoidance. If, for example, meeting Mom's or Dad's date represents a special stress, it's probably a good idea for Mom or Dad to meet casual dates outside the home. For unavoidable situations, such as criticism or embarrassment, one of the four following strategies will be appropriate.

*Restructuring.* Often, altering or restructuring an event can reduce its stress potential. Barbara Davido used this technique to make morning leavetakings less anxiety-provoking for her 7-year-old Luke. Reasoning that the fewer little stresses Luke had to face in the morning, the better he'd handle the big stress of saying goodbye, Barbara made two important changes in her son's morning routine. She moved Luke's wake-up time back fifteen minutes so he wouldn't feel so rushed, and she moved clothes selection, a big time-consumer in the morning, to the evening. Luke's anxiety has not completely vanished, but since Barbara instituted these changes, his goodbyes are much less likely to be accompanied by tears or tantrums.

Other high-stress situations and events that can be restructured include:

• *Big events.* Much of the anxiety could be eliminated if the night before a big event, bedtime is made a little earlier. On the day of the event, the child should schedule his time so that he has fifteen minutes or a half-hour to prepare himself mentally before the big moment.

• *Waiting.* Bringing a book or magazine along is a very simple way to assuage the frustration Type A boys and girls feel when caught in traffic with Mom or Dad or waiting for the school bus.

• *Attending a party.* Suggest to the Type A that he arrive a little early and go with a friend. Then, when he walks in the door, he won't feel as if two dozen pairs of eyes are scrutinizing only him.

*Self-talk.* Often, what makes a situation or event stressful for a child is that it pushes his buttons in a special way. The button may be an expectation or belief about himself, or it may be a perception he has about the other people involved in the situation. For example, many Type A's find criticism especially upsetting, not because they hate being corrected, but because it pushes their perfection button. Criticism means you aren't the perfect person you want to be and if you aren't perfect, other people may not like and respect you.

The goal of self-talk is to identify and correct such stress-producing beliefs, expectations, and perceptions. To illustrate how it works: Say, that the Type A finds classmate Jimmy's presence a stress. Before doing anything else, a parent and child have to discover why Jimmy is a stress. Here, the listening skills I described in chapter 9 will be useful. Is it because Jimmy is a bully, or because Jimmy knows how to get your child's goat in a way no one else does? Or is it because, being very bright, Jimmy intimidates him?

Once parent and child have identified why Jimmy is a source of special discomfort, the next step is to help the Type A develop some reassuring and calming thoughts he can use to maintain his cool in Jimmy's presence. For example, if it turns out that Jimmy is a special stress because he knows how to get your child's goat one such thought might be: "I don't like Jimmy, but I'm not going to give him the satisfaction of knowing he gets on my nerves. I'll just ignore him and go about my business."

Following are some other examples of how self-talk can be used to defuse high-stress situations:

For the Type A who finds criticism especially stressful: "Everyone makes mistakes, but it's a normal part of growing up. No one will think less of me for making a mistake."

For the Type A who finds test-taking stressful: "The world won't come to an end if I don't get the grade I want on this test. All I can do is try my best."

For the Type A who becomes upset when his hand isn't acknowledged: "Teacher isn't deliberately ignoring me. I was called on twice this week. It's a classmate's turn now."

*Prioritizing.* This technique is particularly effective for Type A's who, like Larry Swayze, feel themselves chronically falling behind schedule. When Amanda Swayze told me about her son's problem, she blamed it on overambition. "Larry tries to do too much," she said. And indeed, a few days later, when I went over Larry's schedule with him, I found that he never set fewer than ten daily goals. I also found that his sense of chronically falling behind was due not to the number of his daily goals but to his habit of giving each goal equal weight.

This practice almost always creates a terrible sense of time urgency because it deprives the child of flexibility. If he finds himself running late, he can't say to himself, "I guess I'll have to skip the *Bill Cosby Show* tonight," because, like every other goal in his daily schedule, seeing Cosby is a high priority. So he proceeds to spend the next three or four hours rushing through the other things he has to do, all the while growing more anxious about whether he'll be finished in time to be in front of the TV set at eight o'clock.

Why do Type A's like Larry create such time prisons for themselves? Partly out of compulsiveness—even positive Type A's have a desire to do everything—but the time prison also arises from inexperience. The child hasn't yet learned how to prioritize his daily goals. One way to teach him is by going over your daily schedule with him, pointing out which items are essential, and why (arriving at work on time, for example); and which aren't, and why (picking up clothes from the cleaners). Now, have your Type A write down all the things he plans to do tomorrow in order of importance. Next go over his list with him, and explain why some of his goals should be high priority (school, chores), and others low priority (watching TV, talking to a friend on the phone). You'll probably have to repeat this process several times before the child develops the ability to prioritize on his own. But as he does, you'll find that he adopts a new and much more relaxed attitude toward time.

One cautionary note. Your child won't always agree with your ranking of priorities, so leave him some room for disagreement.

*Pleasure breaks.* Stresses encountered early in the day when energy levels are high often can be easily navigated, but as the day wears on and energy levels wear down, the Type A becomes increasingly vulnerable to his high-strung temperament. Scheduling pleasure breaks at strategic points throughout the day rebuilds depleted energy reserves, allowing the Type A to deal as effectively with afternoon and evening stresses as he does with morning ones.

How many breaks are appropriate, as well as the nature of their content, will vary from child to child. As a general rule, three fifteen- to thirty-minute breaks, scheduled during lunch periods, upon returning home from school, and in the early evening, should be sufficient to keep the Type A's energy at optimum levels throughout the day. The breaks should involve an activity the Type A enjoys and finds relaxing. For some children, this may be reading a book; for others, working on a stamp or baseball-card collection; and for others, talking with a special friend.

Your Type A won't have any trouble deciding how he wants to use these breaks. When it comes to fun things to do, children are full of good ideas. Just be sure your youngster's choices are as specific as possible. A resolution to read a specific book is much more likely to be followed than a vague intention to read a book. Practicality is another criterion to keep in mind when planning pleasure breaks. A practical lunch-break activity is a few minutes of play on the schoolyard jungle gym; an impractical activity is stamp collecting, since the child would have to bring his stamps to school.

### THE RELAXATION RESPONSE

The Relaxation Response is designed to alleviate anxieties, frustrations, and other problematic emotions that don't yield to other stress-management techniques. Created by Dr. Herbert Benson of Harvard University, the response is also a general relaxant, which the Type A can use to soothe himself at the end of a stressful day.

Its three major building blocks are muscle awareness, diaphragmatic breathing, and visual imagery. The response can't be mastered without a knowledge of each, so let's begin by examining them.

#### *Muscle Awareness*

This technique involves progressively tensing and untensing all the major muscle groups. Its purpose is to help a child develop a kind of stress early-warning system by heightening his awareness to the feeling of a tensed muscle, and to show him how to relax stressed muscles. We know from biofeedback experiments that many seemingly involuntary body functions (like blood pressure and muscle tension) can be regulated by the conscious mind.

Repeated two times a week, the following exercises will promote this regulatory mechanism. All you need in order to conduct them is a quiet room and a chair; once the child is seated, tell him to take a deep breath, relax, and think of nothing but your instructions for the next few minutes.

*Legs and feet.* Begin by asking him to elevate his left leg and stretch it outward. Wait ten or fifteen seconds, then ask him if the muscles above and below his knee feel tense. (They will, because they are supporting his outstretched leg.) When he replies "yes," have him put his leg down and direct his attention to how these muscles feel when relaxed. Repeat the exercise with the right leg.

Next, ask the child to grind the ball of his left foot into the ground as if he were squashing a bug. Wait five or ten seconds, then ask him to notice how tense his foot muscles feel. Once the foot has been relaxed, ask him how it feels now. Repeat this exercise with the right foot.

*Abdomen.* Tell the child to sit very upright in the chair, arch his back, and suck in his abdomen as far as possible. Do his stomach and lower-back muscles feel uncomfortable? Encourage him to contrast this unpleasant sensation with the way those muscles feel when relaxed.

*Shoulders.* Now, ask the child to imagine he is a butterfly closing his wings. Tell him to push his shoulder blades as close together as he can. Wait ten or fifteen seconds, then tell him to relax. Next, announce that you have another exercise. This time, you want him to hunch his shoulders up as far as he can and hold them stationary until you count to ten. As in other exercises, the child's attention should be drawn to the way his muscles feel when tensed and when relaxed.

*Arms and fingers.* First, have the child extend his right arm outward. Wait a few seconds, then ask him to notice how hard his forearms and biceps are working to keep his arm extended. How do his forearm and biceps feel when his arm is in a relaxed position? Repeat this exercise with the left arm.

Next, ask the child to spread the fingers of his right hand as far apart as he can. Does he feel each finger quivering with tension? Does he notice how different his fingers feel when relaxed? Repeat this exercise with the fingers of the left hand.

*Head and neck.* Have the child extend his neck upward as far as he can, then relax it. Next, have him tilt his head as far to the left and right as he can, then forward and backward. As in other exercises, he should be asked how his muscles feel when tensed and when relaxed.

*Facial muscles.* Ask the child to clench his jaws until you've counted to fifteen. Next, have him open his mouth as wide as he can until you've again counted to fifteen. Repeat this procedure with the forehead muscles. Make the child knit them as tightly as he can. How did these muscles feel tensed, then relaxed?

As his experience grows, your child will develop the ability to scan his muscles without going through each of these individual steps.

### Diaphragmatic Breathing

Proper breathing technique is one of the easiest ways to calm oneself. So, in addition to being a building block of the Relaxation Response, like muscle awareness, diaphragmatic breathing gives a child another way of dealing with stress.

Watch a baby, and you'll have a good idea of what such breathing involves. The infant partially breathes in long, slow, deep, rhythmic breaths, using the diaphragm to expand the lungs. This pattern, which brings air down into the lungs, appears to facilitate self-calming. In most modern high-pressure societies, even toddlers and preschoolers display a sharp, shallow, chest-only breathing pattern characteristic of stressed individuals.

Relearning the slow, deep pattern of infancy is the goal of the following exercises, which should be practiced for ten to fifteen minutes twice a day for optimum mastery.

*Slow breathing.* Begin by asking the child to inhale and exhale as deeply as he can. Have him repeat this exercise four or five times. As he inhales and exhales, keep an eye on his diaphragm and rib cage. If he's doing the exercise properly, both should move when he breathes.

*Hold breath.* Next, have the child breathe normally for a minute or two, then ask him to inhale deeply and hold the air in until you count to five. Now, have him exhale as fully as he can. Repeat this exercise four or five times. Again, pay attention to his rib cage and diaphragm.

*Fat and skinny breathing.* In moments of stress and tension, a child will unconsciously revert to the short, shallow breathing pattern. By heightening his awareness of the differences between chest- and diaphragm-based breathing, this technique helps him spot the reversion. Diaphragmatic awareness is heightened by fat breathing. Ask the child to inhale as much air as possible, while simultaneously making his belly as fat as he can. (This exercise works the diaphragm to the maximum.) Count to five, then tell him to breathe out as deeply as he can. Awareness of chest-only inhalation is enhanced by skinny breathing. Ask the child to inhale while simultaneously sucking in his stomach. Again, count to five and tell him to exhale as hard as he can. At the end of the exercise, which should be repeated three or four times, it's a good idea to ask the child to describe fat and skinny breathing. Thinking about this question will heighten the child's awareness of the different feelings each produces.

### Visual Imaging

Unlike diaphragmatic breathing and muscle awareness, which relax the mind by relaxing the body, visual imagery works directly on the mind. It uses pleasant images, thoughts, and memories to soothe anxieties, frustrations, and fears. Younger children in particular are likely to have trouble grasping how a thought can alter a feeling, so, in introducing the technique to a child 9 years old or younger, it's a good idea to demonstrate the phenomenon to him.

You can do this by asking the child to close his eyes and think of a recent incident like, for instance, the day he knocked over his sister's birthday cake. How did he feel when he saw the cake on the floor? Embarrassed. How does he feel now, thinking about the incident? Still a little embarrassed.

Next, ask him to think of some relaxing places and things. The purpose of this exercise is to create a store of thoughts and feelings that he can draw on during visual imaging. If he can't think of any relaxing situations, here are three he can use during practice sessions.

• He is lying on the beach. The sun above him feels radiantly warm, the sand beneath him soft and inviting. The only sound he can hear is the gentle splashing of waves along the shore. He feels very relaxed and calm.

• He is walking through a beautiful forest where the only sound is the gentle whoosh of a waterfall flowing somewhere in the distance. It is a warm day, but the canopy of trees overhead makes him feel pleasantly cool.

• It is a lazy Sunday morning. Everyone else is asleep. A cool rain beats a gentle tattoo on his bedroom window. The child is under the covers feeling soft and snuggly and a little sleepy.

It may take as long as one to two months of twice-weekly practice sessions before such images begin to acquire the power to soothe and relax. But you can optimize the relaxation process by following these rules during practice sessions:

• Find the right time and setting. The right time is when the house is quiet (although a little soft background music may be appropriate). The right setting is a place where the child feels relaxed; the right position, one he feels comfortable in.

• Before beginning a practice session, have the child close his eyes, take several deep breaths, then scan his body for tensed muscles.

• Once relaxed, he's ready to begin imagining. During the first week or two of practice, this process will feel strange to him. It's often a good idea for a parent to begin each session by verbally painting a picture of a relaxing scene.

• Four to five minutes should be devoted to the imagining process itself. If the child complains of boredom, quietly tell him: "I'm glad you noticed. It's important to know how to set the pace. That is the first step. Next time, we can go longer if you like."

## THE RELAXATION RESPONSE

This technique, which combines all the child has learned about imagery, breathing, and muscle awareness into a single, unified antistress response, grew out of an observation by Dr. Herbert Benson. Studying people in meditative states, Dr. Benson noticed that they experienced the exact opposite of a stress response. Instead of quickening, their breathing slowed, and instead of increasing, their muscle tension decreased. He also found that during meditation, the brain produces long, loping alpha waves instead of short, tense beta waves.

Dr. Benson named this antistress state the Relaxation Response and developed an eight-step procedure to evoke it. Suitable for individuals of all ages, the response can be elicited in one or two minutes with experience. It gives a child an alternative way of dealing with emotionally charged situations that don't yield to stress-management techniques.

In practicing the procedure, have the child rehearse the technique's eight steps in the following sequence:

• Begin by having him close his eyes and clear his mind. If he has trouble ridding himself of unwanted thoughts, suggest that he imagine himself able to zap them away with a laser gun.

• Next, tell him to take two or three deep, long, diaphragm-based breaths.

• To further relax himself, ask the child to feel if he has tensed muscles.

• Now, have him do two slow headrolls and two slow shoulder rolls. (Head roll: move head down to chest, then move it toward one shoulder, then the other. Shoulder roll: make circles forward and backward with shoulders.)

• Ask him to slowly repeat the phrase "I am calm" two or three times.

• Have him take several more slow, deep breaths.

• Praise him quietly and frequently.

• Now, ask him to slowly open his eyes, and as he does, have him repeat this phrase: "I am feeling alert and calm."


NUTRITION

Although nutrition isn't the stress cure-all some food experts claim it to be, by promoting a general sense of well-being, a proper diet can materially enhance a child's (or an adult's) ability to handle anxiety, frustration, and fear.

What constitutes such a diet?

I believe the soundest thinking on nutrition can be found in the U.S. government's Recommended Daily Allowances, which declare the following six nutrients to be essential to physical *and* emotional well-being. The parent who ensures that her Type A gets his RDA of each item on the list (since RDAs vary according to age, sex, weight, and activity level, check with your pediatrician to find out what your youngster's are) may not see the dramatic results promised by nutritionists, who believe diet is a kind of magic antistress bullet, but she will find him better able to control his high-strung temperament.

The six nutrients are:

*Water* is important because it is the principal ingredient in all body fluids, including blood, urine, and sweat, as well as the main component of all cells. Six 8-fluid-ounce servings is the RDA for people of all ages. However, some of our water intake is provided by the foods we eat.

*Carbohydrates.* A major source of energy, carbohydrates can be found in starchy foods such as bananas, breads, cereals, grains, milk, and fruits, as well as sugar and molasses.

*Fats.* Butter, margarine, cream, egg yolks, whole milk, vegetable oils, salad dressings, and mayonnaise are all rich in this substance, which, in addition to being a major energy source, also plays an important role in cell production.

*Protein.* Fish, poultry, lean meat, and milk are all good sources of protein, which is a major source of energy as well as a key element in cell and tissue construction.

*Minerals.* The four major substances in this category—sodium, calcium, phosphorous, and iron—each serve the body in major ways. Sodium, which is found in salt, cheese, milk, shellfish, and eggs, is important in maintaining the body's fluid balance. Calcium is a key building block of bones and teeth, and can be obtained from milk and milk products, green vegetables, sardines, and bean curds. Phosphorous also is essential to maintaining strong, healthy teeth; milk and milk products are a rich source of this mineral. Iron is abundant in liver, eggs, lean beef, dried beans, lentils, veal, poultry, tuna, sardines, peanuts, and dark, leafy vegetables. Iron is essential because it combines with protein to create hemoglobin, the substance that allows the blood to deliver oxygen to the tissues.

*Vitamins.* In the simplest sense, vitamins aren't nutrients at all, but catalysts that allow nutrients to make their individual contributions to the body's well-being. Without vitamins, protein, fats, and minerals would pass through the body undigested. Of the six key vitamins, vitamin A, found in green leafy vegetables, fruits, margarine or butter, and liver, plays the most important role in maintaining skin tone and vision. The

B-complex vitamins also play a key role in their maintenance, as well as in promoting healthy hair. They include thiamin ($B_1$), riboflavin ($B_2$), niacin ($B_3$), pyridoxamine ($B_6$), and biotin, folic acid, and cobalamine ($B_{12}$).

Vitamin D helps the body utilize calcium and phosphorous, the two key building blocks of strong teeth and bones. It can be obtained from fortified milk, fish-liver oils, certain fish such as tuna, herring, and salmon, and from the sun's rays upon the skin.

Vitamin E is a kind of warehouse vitamin. It enhances the body's ability to store other vitamins, as well as unsaturated fats. This vitamin, which can be found in butter or margarine, whole-grain breads, cereal grains, and vegetables, also is important for cell growth.

Vitamin K facilitates the blood's ability to clot and thus is a key ingredient in the healing process. It can be found in cereals, leafy vegetables, and, to a lesser extent, in cereals, fruits, and dairy products.

Although fiber is the part of food not digested by the body, it plays an essential role in maintaining the health of the intestinal tract. In addition, recent studies have shown that a high-fiber diet can be an important factor in reducing the risk of colon cancer and heart disease.

Unlike these six nutrients, which enhance the ability to resist stress, caffeine and sugar actually produce stresslike reactions in the body. An 8-year-old Type A bounces around the kitchen after a breakfast of sugar-coated cereal, and a 16-year-old seems to levitate out of his chair after a second cup of morning coffee, not because they are high-strung, but because these substances are stimulants, which produce a "wired" reaction in any child. While a good sound breakfast is the key meal of the day for all of us, young and old alike, sugar-rich cereals have no place in the diet of an 8-year-old. He can get all the sugar he needs from fruits such as bananas and cantaloupes. Nor is coffee good for a 16-year-old.

One last point about nutrition and stress. Rapid eating can indirectly make the body more vulnerable to stress because it hinders the digestive system's ability to break down nutrients into an easily absorbable form. And the fewer nutrients a child absorbs, the less resistance he has to stress. What makes this point particularly pertinent to the Type A is that, like everything else he does, he likes to eat rapidly. Creating a relaxed atmosphere with small talk is one way to encourage a slower dining pace. It is also a good idea to eliminate distractions such as TV, magazines, or books.

### EXERCISE

If you exercise regularly, you already know what an effective antistress agent it is. Constant movement produces physiological changes, which can help calm the most frayed nerves and produce an overall sense of well-being. A disappointing grade or an upcoming test looks a lot different after a swim or a bike ride. Exercise has some other special benefits for the Type A boy and girl. One is related to heart disease. Studies show that aerobic exercise, in particular, can regulate blood pressure and improve cardiac function. In addition, the sense of mastery and self-confidence exercise confers can help boost the A's self-esteem.

Unfortunately, none of these benefits will sound very persuasive to a Type A who has sedentary impulses. How do you get a boy or girl who isn't so inclined to take up a regular exercise program? Here are some suggestions:

*Tailor the activity to the child.* Be sure to factor in age when helping a boy or girl find a sport. Children ages 7, 8, and 9 are much more likely to stick to team sports, such as baseball, basketball, and soccer, than to individual sports such as swimming; which require a high level of discipline. Tailoring also involves finding a sport that matches the child's talents and inclinations. For older youngsters who prefer to set their own challenges, personal sports such as running, weight training, and swimming will be most appropriate. Team sports will be best for boys and girls who are more outgoing and enjoy playing a leadership role.

*Set a good example.* You can't expect an 8-, 10-, or 12-year-old to develop the discipline and motivation to adhere to a regular program of physical exercise in a home where the principal parental leisure activities are watching TV and snacking. If you want your child to exercise regularly, you need to provide him with a role model.

*Develop a family fitness program.* One excellent way to get a child involved in regular exercise is by making exercise a family affair. Biking, hiking, volleyball—there are a number of sports that are not only a healthy way for everyone to have fun, but that also can bring the family closer together.

*Start slowly.* Exercise is a physical stress, and if your child is like most American children today—out of shape—he'll need time to acclimate his body to the demands of a physical regimen. Aerobic sports, such as bike riding, running, and swimming, could be introduced with three quarter-hour sessions per week, then gradually build up to thirty- or sixty-minute sessions. If your youngster is overweight or has any health problems, consult your pediatrician before inaugurating an exercise program.

An added benefit of exercise is that it can help strengthen a child's self-confidence. Watching the seconds fall off of his mile or his prowess at the plate grow gives him new reason to feel good about himself. The ability to overcome an unruly temper or a paralyzing anxiety can further enhance a youngster's sense of mastery and competence. Which is why exercise, like stress management and the other techniques in this chapter, can help boost your Type A's self-esteem.

The most important source of self-esteem, though, is you. And if this book can be said to have had a single aim, it's been to show you how to build the strong, secure sense of self that will allow your child to be all that a Type A can be.

—

# BIBLIOGRAPHY

*General References:*

*Type A Behavior Pattern—Research, Theory, and Intervention.* Editors: B. Kent Houston and G. R. Snyder. New York: John Wiley and Sons, 1938.

*Ibid,* chapter 6. "Exploring the Type A Behavior Pattern in Children and Adolescents." Carl E. Thoresen and Jerry R. Patillo, pp. 98–145.

*Trusting Heart: Great News About Type A Behavior.* Redford Williams, M.D. New York: Times Books, 1989.

*Treating Type A Behavior and Your Heart.* Meyer Friedman, M.D., and Diane Ulmer, R.N., M.S. New York: Knopf, 1984.

*Values Clarification. A Handbook of Practical Strategies for Teachers and Students.* Sidney B. Simon, Leland W. Howe, and Howard Kirschenbaum. New York: A&W Publishers, 1972.

*Stress Management for the Healthy Type A—Theory and Practice.* Ethel Roskies. New York: Guilford Press, 1987.


*Specific References:*

Ainsworth, M.D.S., and B. Wittig (1969). "Attachment and Exploratory Behavior of One-Year-Olds in a Strange Situation." In B. Foss (ed.), *Determinants of Infant Behavior*, vol. 4. London: Methuen 9.

Bergman, L. R., and D. Magnusson (1986). "Type A Behavior: A Longitudinal Study from Childhood to Adulthood." *Psychosomatic Medicine* 48(1–2), pp. 134–42.

Bishop, E. G., B. J. Hailey, and H. N. Anderson (1987). "Assessment of Type A Behavior in Children: A Comparison of Two Instruments." *Journal of Human Stress* 13, pp. 121–27.

Booth-Kewley, S., and H. S. Friedman (1987). "Psychological Predictors of Heart Disease: A Quantitative Review." *Psychological Bulletin* 101, pp. 343–62.

Bortner, R. W., R. H. Rosenman, and M. Friedman (1970). Familial Similarity in Pattern A Behavior: Fathers and Sons." *Journal of Chronic Diseases* 23, p. 3943.

Bracke, P. E. (1986). "Parental Childrearing Practices and the Development of Type A Behavior in Children." Doctoral dissertation, Stanford University.

Butensky, A., V. Faralli, D. Heebner, and I. Waldron (1976). "Elements of the Coronary-Prone Behavior Pattern in Children and Teenagers." *Journal of Psychosomatic Research* 20, 439–44.

Corrigan, S. A., and D. S. Moskowitz (1983). "Type A Behavior in Preschool Children: Construct Validation Evidence for the MYTH." *Child Development* 54, pp. 1513–21.

Eagleston, J. R., K. Kirmil-Gray, C. E. Thoresen, S. A. Wiedenfeld, P. Bracke, L. Heft, and B. Arnow (1986). "Physical Health Correlates of Type A Behavior in Children and Adolescents." *Journal of Behavioral Medicine* 9, pp. 341–62.

Fontana, A., and J. F. Davidio (1984). "The Relationship Between Stressful Life Events and School-Related Performances of Type A and Type B Adolescents." *Journal of Human Stress* 10 (1), pp. 50–55.

Friedman, H. S., and S. Booth-Kewley (1987a). "The 'disease-prone personality': A Meta-analytic View of the Construct." *American Psychologist* 42, pp. 539–55.

——— (1987b). "Personality, Type A Behavior, and Coronary Heart Disease: The Role of Emotional Expression." *Journal of Personality and Social Psychology* 53, pp. 783–92.

Friedman, M., C. E. Thoresen, J. J. Gill, D. Ulmer, L. H. Powell, V. A. Price, B. Brown, L. Thompson, D. D. Rubin, W. S.

Breall, E. Bourg, R. Levy, and T. Dixon (1986). "Alteration of Type A Behavior and Its Effect on Cardiac Recurrences in Postmyocardial Infarction Patients: Summary Result of the Recurrent Coronary Prevention Project." *American Heart Journal* 112 (4), pp. 653–65.

John W. Gastorf, Jerry Suls, and Glenn S. Sanders (1980). "Type A Coronary-Prone Behavior Pattern and Social Facilitation." *Journal of Personality and Social Psychology* 38 (5), 773–80.

Glueck, C. J. (1986). "Pediatric Primary Prevention of Atherosclerosis." *New England Journal of Medicine* 314 (3), 175–77.

Heft, L., C. E. Thoresen, K. Kirmil-Gray, S. A.Wiedenfeld, J. R. Eagleston, P. Bracke, and B. Arnow (in press). "Emotional and Temperamental Correlates of Type A in Children and Adolescents." *Journal of Youth & Adolescence.*

Hunter, S. M., T. M. Wolf, M. C. Sklov, L. S. Webber, R. M. Watson, and G. S. Berenson (1982). "Type A Coronary-Prone Behavior Pattern and Cardiovascular Risk Factor Variables in Children and Adolescents: The Bogalusa Heart Study." *Journal of Chronic Disease,* 35 (8), pp. 613–20.

Jennings, J. R., and K. A. Matthews (1984). "The Impatience of Youth: Phasic Cardiovascular Response in Type A and Type B Elementary School-Age Boys." *Psychosomatic Medicine* 46 (6), pp. 498–511.

Karen, Robert (1990). "Becoming Attached." *The Atlantic Monthly,* pp. 35–70. Jan. 90.

Kelly, Kevin R., and Gerald L. Stone, (1987). "Effects of Three Psychological Treatments and Self-Monitoring on the Reduction of Type A Behavior." *Journal of Counseling Psychology* 34 (1), pp. 46–54.

Kirmil-Gray, K. J. R. Eagleston, C. E. Thoresen, L. Heft, B. Arnow, and P. Bracke, (in press). "Developing Measures of Type A Behavior in Children and Adolescents." *Journal of Human Stress.*

Krantz, D. S., U. Lundberg, and M. Frankenhaeuser (1987). Stress and Type A behavior: Interactions between environmental and biological factors. In A. R. Baum and J. E. Singer (eds.), *Handbook of Psychology and Health,* vol. 5. "Stress and Coping." Hillsdale, NJ: Erlbaum.

B. W. Lake, E. C. Suarez, N. Schneiderman, and N. Tocci (1985).

"The Type A Behavior Pattern, Physical Fitness, and Psychophysiological Reactivity." *Health Psychology,* 4 (2), pp. 169–87.

K. A. Lawler, M. T. Allen, E. C. Critcher, and B. A. Standard (1981). "The Relationshp of Physiological Responses to the Coronary-Prone Behavior Pattern in Children." *Journal of Behavioral Medicine* 4 (2), pp. 203–16.

Lundberg, U. (1983a). "Note on Type A Behavior and Cardiovascular Responses to Challenge in 3–6-Year-Old Children." *Journal of Psychosomatic Research* 27 (1), pp. 39–42.

——— (in press). "Stress and Type A Behavior in Children." *Journal of American Academy of Child Psychiatry.*

D. T. Manning, P. M. Balson, S. M. Hunter, G. S. Berenson, and A. S. Willis (1987). "Comparison of the Prevalence of Type A Behavior in Boys and Girls from Two Contrasting Socioeconomic Status Groups." *Journal of Human Stress* 13, pp. 116–20.

Margolis, L. H., K. R. McLeroy, C. W. Runyan, and B. H. Kaplan (1983). "Type A Behavior: An Ecological Approach." *Journal of Behavioral Medicine* 6, pp. 245–58.

Matthews, K. A. (1977). "Caregiver-Child Interactions and the Type A Coronary-Prone Behavior Pattern." *Child Development* 48, pp. 1752–56.

——— (1979). "Efforts to Control by Children and Adults with Type A Coronary-Prone Behavior Pattern." *Child Development* 50, pp. 842–47.

——— (1982). "Psychological Perspectives on the Type A Behavior Pattern. *Psychological Bulletin* 91, pp. 293–323.

———, and J. Angulo (1980). "Measurement of the Type A Behavior Pattern in Children: Assessment of Children's Competitiveness, Impatience-Anger, and Aggression." *Child Development* 51, pp. 466–75.

———, and N. E. Avis (1983). "Stability of Overt Type A Behaviors in Children: Results from a One-Year Longitudinal Study." *Child Development* 54 (6), pp. 1507–12.

———, and S. G. Haynes (1986). "Type A Behavior Pattern and Coronary Disease Risk." *American Journal of Epidemiology* 123 (6), pp. 923–59.

———, and J. R. Jennings, (1984). "Cardiovascular Responses of

Boys Exhibiting the Type A Behavior Pattern." *Psychosomatic Medicine* 46, pp. 484–97.

———, and D. S. Krantz (1976). "Resemblance of Twins and Their Parents in Pattern A Behavior." *Psychosomatic Medicine* 38, pp. 140–44.

———, R. H. Rosenman, T. M. Dembroski, E. Harris, and J. M. MacDougall (1983). "Familial Resemblance in Components of the Type A Behavior Pattern: A Reanalysis of the California Twin Study." Unpublished manuscript.

———, and J. M. Siegel (1982). "The Type A Pattern in Children and Adolescents: Assessment, Development, and Associated Coronary Risk." In A. R. Baum and J. E. Singer (eds.), *Handbook of Psychology and Health* (vol. 2). Hillsdale, NJ: Erlbaum.

——— (1983). "Type A Behaviors for Children, Social Comparison, and Standards for Self-Evaluation. *Developmental Psychology* 19 (1), pp. 135–40.

———, and J. I. Volkin (1981). "Efforts to Excel and the Type A Behavior Pattern in Children. *Child Development* 52, pp. 1283–89.

Muranaka, M., J. D. Lane, E. C. Juarez, N. B. Anderson, J. Suzuki, and R. B. Williams (1988). "Stimulus-Specific Patterns of Cardiovascular Reactivity in Type A & B Subjects: Evidence for Enhanced Vagal Reactivity in Type B. *Psychophysiology* 25, pp. 330–38.

Murray, D. M., S. M. Blake, R. Prineas, and R. F. Gillum (1985). "Cardiovascular Responses in Type A Children During a Cognitive Challenge." *Journal of Behavioral Medicine* 8 (4), pp. 377–95.

———, K. A. Matthews, S. M. Blake, R. J. Prineas, and R. F. Gillum, (1986). "Type A Behavior in Children: Demographic, Behavioral, and Physiological Correlates." *Health Psychology* 5 (2), pp. 159–69.

Murray, J. L., J. G. Bruhn, and H. Bunce (1983). "Assessment of Type A Behavior in Preschoolers." *Journal of Human Stress* 9 (3), pp. 32–39.

Newman, W. P., D. S. Freedman, A. W. Voors, P. D. Gard, S. S. Srinivasan, J. L. Cresanta, G. D. Williamson, L. S. Webber, and G. S. Berenson (1986). "Relation of Lipoprotein Levels and Systolic Blood Pressure to Early Atherosclerosis." *New England Journal of Medicine* 314, pp. 138–44.

Nunes, E. V., K. A. Frank, and D. S. Kornfeld (1987). "Psychologic Treatment for Type A Behavior Pattern and for Coronary Heart Disease. A Meta-analysis of the Literature." *Psychosomatic Medicine* 48, pp. 159–73.

Parker, F. C., D. W. Harsha, R. P. Farris, L. S. Webber, G. C. Frank, and G. S. Berenson (1986). "Reducing the Risk of Cardiovascular Disease in Children." In K. Holroyd and T. L. Creer (eds.), *Self-Management of Chronic Disease*. New York: Academic Press.

Parkes, C. M., and J. Stevenson-Hinde, (eds.) (1982). *The Place of Attachment in Human Behavior*. New York: Basic Books.

Powell, L., and C. E. Thoresen, (1987). "Modifying the Type A Behavior Pattern: A Small Group Treatment Approach." In J. A. Blumenthal and D. C. McKee (eds.), *Applications of Behavioral Medicine and Health Psychology: A Clinician's Sourcebook* (vol. 1). Sarasota, FL: Professional Resource Exchange.

Rahe, R. H., L. Hervig, and R. H. Rosenman (1978). "The Heritability of Type A Behavior." *Psychosomatic Medicine* 40, pp. 478–86.

Siegel, J. M. (1982). "Type A Behavior and Self-Reports of Cardiovascular Arousal in Adolescents." *Journal of Human Stress* 8 (3), pp. 24–30.

Siegel, J. M. (1984). "Anger and Cardiovascular Risk in Adolescents." *Health Psychology* 3 (4), pp. 293–13.

———, and C. J. Leitch, (1981). "Assessment of the Type A Behavior Pattern in Adolescents." *Psychosomatic Medicine* 43 (1), pp. 45–56.

———, K. A. Matthews, and C. J. Leitch, (1981). "Validation of the Type A Interview Assessment of Adolescents: A Multidimensional Approach." *Psychosomatic Medicine* 43 (4), pp. 311–21.

——— (1983). "Blood Pressure Variability and the Type A Behavior Pattern in Adolescence." *Journal of Psychosomatic Research* 27 (4), pp. 265–72.

Steinberg, L. (1987). "Stability (and Instability) of Type A Behavior from Children to Young Adulthood." *Developmental Psychology* 22, pp. 393–402.

Thoresen, C. E., and A. Ohman (1987). "The Type A Behavior Pattern: "A Person-Environment Interaction Perspective." In D. Magnusson and A. Ohman (eds.), *Psychopathology: An Interaction Perspective*. New York: Academic Press.

Waldron, I., A. Hickey, C. McPherson, A. Butensky, L. Gruss, K. Overall, A. Schmader, and D. Wohlmuth (1980). "Type A Behavior Pattern: Relationship to Variation in Blood Pressure, Parental Characteristics, and Academic and Social Activities of Students." *Journal of Human Stress* 6, pp. 16–27.

Webber, L. S., J. L. Cresanta, A. W. Voors, and G. S. Berenson (1983). "Tracking of Cardiovascular Disease-Risk Factors Variables in School-Aged Children." *Journal of Chronic Diseases* 36, pp. 647–60.

Weidner, G., R. McLellarn, G. Sexton, J. Istvan, and S. Connor (1987). "Type A Behavior and Physiologic Coronary Risk Factors in Children of the Family Heart Study: Results from a 1-Year Follow-up." *Psychosomatic Medicine* 48, pp. 480–88.

———, G. Sexton, J. D. Matarazzo, and R. Friend (1988). "Type A Behavior in Children, Adolescents, and Their Parents." *Developmental Psychology* 24 (1), pp. 118–21.

Whalen, C. K., and B. Henker, (1986). "Type A Behavior in Normal and Hyperactive Children: Multisource Evidence of Overlapping Constructs." *Child Development* 57, pp. 688–99.

Williams, R. B., J. C. Barefoot, and R. B. Shekelle (1985). "The Health Consequences of Hostility." In M. Chesney and R. Rosenman (eds.), *Anger and Hostility in Cardiovascular and Behavioral Disorders*. New York: Hemisphere.

Wolf, T. M., S. M. Hunter, L. S. Webber, and G. S. Berenson (1981). "Self-Concept, Focus of Control, Goal Blockage, and Coronary-Prone Behavior Pattern in Children and Adolescents: Bogalusa Heart Study." *Journal of General Psychology* 105, pp. 13–26.

# INDEX

Acceptance, parental, 136–42, 143, 147
Accumulation, 168, 170
Achievement striving, 22, 23, 26, 35, 44, 52, 59, 64, 71, 87, 94, 97, 168, 170, 173
Acting out behavior, 36, 128, 142, 146
Adultification, 50, 75–76, 80–87
Aerobic exercise, 198, 199
Aggression, 100, 158, 168, 170
Altruism, 88, 90, 168
Ambition. *See* Achievement striving
Anger and hostility, 6, 9, 35, 41
  authoritarian discipline and, 155–56
  biological component to, 24
  communication about, 145–46, 148–49
  elements of, 101
  heart disease risk and, 27–28, 45, 91–94, 97–99
  parental, defense against, 113–14
  in peer relationships, 24, 32, 41, 100
  physiological response in, 92–94, 99–100
  self-directed, 24, 101, 113
  self-esteem and, 23, 24
Anxiety
  free-floating, 28
  internalized, 50
  performance, 26, 34–36, 126–27, 151
  school, 157
  *See also* Stress

Athletics
  coach relationship in, 62–65
  critical parent and, 45
  defeat in, coping with, 129–30
  and leadership model, 174
  overencouraging parent and, 111–12
  role models in, 89, 174
  stress management and, 198–99
Attachment disruption, insecurity and, 16, 69–70
Attention-getting behavior, 165–66, 170
Attribution, hostile, 100
Authoritarian discipline. *See* Discipline, authoritarian
Autonomy, 170, 173–74

Benson, Herbert, 190, 194–95
Bergman, Lars, 23
Blood pressure, 10, 27, 45, 92, 100
Body language, parental, 141–42
Bracke, Paul, 32–33, 37–38, 155
Brazelton, T. Berry, 76, 86
Breathing technique, 192–93
Brooks, Andrée, 89

Caffeine, stress reaction to, 197
Carbohydrates, in diet, 196
Caregiver relationship, 19–20, 34, 65–67
Cheating, 45–46

Child-centered communication, 101, 135–54
  accepting listener in, 136–42
  of criticism, 147–51
  listening traps in, 138–40
  of praise, 151–53
  reflective listening in, 142–47
  sympathetic listening in, 116, 128–29, 138
*Children of Fast Track Parents* (Brooks), 89
Cholesterol levels, 27, 45, 92, 100
Coach relationship, 62–65
Cohen, Sara Lee, 38
Comfort index, 16, 24
Communication
  open/honest, 7–8
  parent-centered, 33–34, 36–37, 134–35, 138
  with peers, 37, 133
  about values, 182–83
  *See also* Child-centered communication
Community activities, 8, 182
Comparisons, social, 33, 34, 35, 39, 108, 109–10, 124
Compassion, 88, 90, 171
Competence, 3, 17, 19–20, 49–50
Competitiveness, 6, 25–26, 42–46, 59–60, 71, 94, 97, 158
Compulsiveness, 189
Control needs, 68
Cooperation, 88, 90, 170
Cortisol, 92
Criticism
  alternatives to, 150–51
  checking impulse, 109–10
  child-centered, 147–51
  global, 148–49
  as parenting style, 18, 30, 40–48, 109
  self-esteem and, 148, 149, 161
  stressful, 187–88
Cynicism, 100

Davido, John, 56
Davidson, Sara, 30
Daycare worker relationship, 67–68
Delegation of responsibility, parental, 51–52
Dembroski, Theodore, 99
Depression, 28, 50, 52
Directiveness, parental, 32, 33, 34, 36, 37
Discipline, authoritarian
  critical parent and, 42, 46
  ineffectiveness of, 158–59
  moral myopia and, 155–56

Discipline, respect-oriented, 8, 48, 101, 154–67
  logical consequences in, 163–64, 165
  moral development and, 156, 161–62
  natural consequences in, 161–63, 165
  penalties/punishments in, 164–65
  preventive, 157–61
Disruptive behavior, 62
Distrust, 24, 112
Dominance (leadership), 3, 158, 159, 168, 170, 174
Double messages, 107–08

Eagleton, Jean, 28
Early learning, 30, 39–40, 75–76, 84–87
Eating
  nutrition and, 195–97
  rapid, 197–98
Elkind, David, 50, 76, 80, 84
Empathy, 149, 168, 171
Endurance, 170, 174–75
Epinephrine, 92
Esteem. *See* Self-esteem
Exercise, 198–99
Exhibition, 168, 170
Expectations, high, 35, 50, 108
  caregiver behavior and, 19–20, 65–66, 67
  checking, 114–15
  negative behavior and, 17–18, 21–28
  parental behavior and, 18–19, 119, 127
  perfection need in, 41, 46–47
  success need in, 32, 37
  teacher behavior and, 20, 56, 57, 58, 61
Extracurricular activities, overcommitment to, 26–27, 36, 39–40, 115

Failure, goal, 127–33
Faintness, 28
Family
  activities, 8, 182
  fitness program, 199
  rich life, 81–82, 84
Fats, in diet, 196
Fiber, in diet, 197
Field, Tiffany, 7, 23, 169
Fontana, Anna, 56
Friedman, Meyer, 94, 95, 96, 173
Friendship, 72, 170
  *See also* Peer relationship

Genetic factors, comfort index and, 16, 24
Girls, anger in, 24
Global criticism, 148–49

Global superlatives, 151–52
Goals, realistic, 8, 118–33
  failed, 127–33
  implementing, 124–27
  negotiation, 119–24
  REMD approach to, 119
  self-esteem and, 118, 125
Goals, sky-high. *See* Expectations, high

Headaches, 28, 50, 52
Heart disease risk, 4, 6, 10, 88
  anger and, 27–28, 45, 91–94, 97–99
  exercise effect on, 198
  linked to Type A behavior, 95–99
  narcissism and, 90
  self-esteem and, 90, 101
Hecht, Lorna, 28
Hecker, Barbara, 70
Hidden messages, listening for, 142–47
Hostile affect, 100
Hostility. *See* Anger and hostility
Hunter, John, 96
*Hurried Child, The* (Elkind), 50, 80, 84
Hurrier style of parenting, 30, 49–54
Hypercompetitiveness. *See*
  Competitiveness

Impatience, 6, 26–27, 36, 94, 116–17
Individuality, acceptance of, 51
Infancy
  attachment disruption in, 16, 69–70
  early learning in, 84–85
Insecurity. *See* Self-esteem
Instructiveness, parental, 35, 37–38
Intensity, parental, 32–33, 34
Intelligence, 3, 17

Kelly, Kevin, 169
Kliewer, Wendy, 42

Lasch, Christopher, 77
Leadership (dominance), 3, 158, 159,
  168, 170, 174
Limit-setting, 159–60
Listening, parental
  accepting, 136–42
  reflective, 142–47
  sympathetic, 116, 128–29, 138
  traps, 138–40
Logical consequences, 163–64, 165
Low-density lipoprotein (LDL), 92, 93

Matthews, Karen, 5, 6, 17
Minerals, food sources of, 196
Modesty, excessive, 72
Moral myopia, 45–46, 155–56
Moral reasoning, 46, 156, 161–62, 175

Multiphasic Risk Intervention Trials
  (MRFIT), 98–99
Muscle relaxation, 190–92
Muscle tension, 28
*My Left Foot*, 84–85

Narcissism, 77, 83, 89–90
Natural consequences, 162–63, 165
Nurturance, 38–39, 53, 68, 168, 170
Nutrition, 195–98

Openness, parental, 51
Opinoid secretion, low, 16, 24
Osler, William, 96
Overcommitment impulse, 26–27, 36,
  39–40, 115
Overencouragement, parental, 18, 65,
  110–12, 119
Overpraise, parental, 18, 112, 119, 151

Panksepp, Jaak, 16
Parental behavior, 10
  checking old habits, 107–17
  critical style of, 30, 40–48, 109
  do-nothing rule of, 125–26
  hurrier style of, 30, 49–54
  role modeling in, 8, 82, 116–17, 169,
    172–75, 198
  sky-high goals and, 6–7, 18–19, 32,
    37, 41, 46–47
  as stress buffer, 81–83, 84
  superachiever style of, 29–40
  *See also* Child-centered communica-
    tion; Communication; Criticism;
    Discipline, authoritarian; Disci-
    pline, respect-oriented; Goals, re-
    alistic; Praise; Stress manage-
    ment
Peer counseling, 181–82
Peer relationship
  communication and, 37, 133
  competitive, 25, 45
  daring/taunting, 73
  expectations, high and, 20
  hostility/distrust, 24, 41, 100
  hypersensitive, 72–73
  moral myopia in, 155
  problem-solving analysis of, 131–32
  reflective listening about, 143–44,
    145
  resentment/ jealousy, 70–72
  sharing feelings about failure of, 133
  social comparisons and, 33, 34, 35, 39
  stressful, 188
Perfection need, parental, 41, 46–47,
  107

Performance
  anxiety, 26, 34–36, 126–27, 151
  impatience and, 27
  *See also* School performance
Perspective building elements, 8–9
Perspective taking strategy, 109–10,
  129, 142, 146–47
Phillips, Kevin, 78
Play/relaxation, 171, 189–90
Point-of-view remarks, 148
*Politics of Rich and Poor, The* (Phillips),
  78
Praise
  blind, 128, 138
  child-centered, 151–53
  double message in, 107–08
  overpraise, 18, 112, 119, 151
  Type A response to, 24, 112
Priortizing technique, 188–89
Projection technique, 110–11
Protein, in diet, 196
Psychological reactivity, 5–6, 23, 184
Psychosomatic complaints, 50, 52
Punishment. *See* Discipline, authoritar-
  ian; Discipline, respect-oriented

Reasonable Expectations Mutually De-
  rived (REMD), 119
Reassurance, parental, 128, 138
Recognition, 171
Recommended Daily Allowances
  (RDAs), 195–96
Reflective listening, 142–47
Relaxation response, 190, 194–95
Reprimands, positive, 161
Role modeling
  parental, 8, 82, 116–17, 169, 172–75,
  198
  societal, 88–89
Rosenman, Ray, 94, 95, 96–97
Roskies, Ethel, 173

Save time impulse, 27
School performance
  anxiety about, 36, 157
  goal implementation and, 125–26
  goal setting and, 121–22
  impatience and, 27, 36
  *See also* Teacher relationship
Self-anger, 24, 101, 113
Self-esteem
  anger and, 23
  attachment disruption and, 16, 69–
  70
  building, 7–8, 101–02, 105
  criticism and, 148, 149, 161

  discipline and, 156, 161
  exercise and, 199
  goal setting and, 118, 125
  heart disease risk and, 90, 101
  overpraise and, 151–52
  parent-oriented communication and,
  36–37
Selfishness, enlightened, 54
Self-talk, 187–88
Sibling relationship
  leadership impulse and, 159
  problematic impulses and, 158–59
Significant others
  expectations of, 19–21
  *See also* Caregiver relationship; Pa-
  rental behavior; Peer relationship; Sibling relationship;
  Teacher relationship
Simon, Sidney, 175
Sleep problems, 28, 32
Social avoidance, 100
Social comparisons, 33, 34, 35, 39, 108,
  109–10, 124
Social goals, 131–32
Society
  adultification of, 50, 75–76, 80–87
  decline of values, 87–90
  success ethic in, 74–75, 76–80
  Type A values and, 7, 8–9, 19, 77
Somatization, 28, 50
Spock, Benjamin, 76
Sports. *See* Athletics
Stomachache, 28, 50, 52
Stress
  buffer, parental, 81–83, 84
  situations causing, 186
  symptoms of, 184–85
  vulnerability to, 184
Stress management, 186–99
  breathing techniques in, 192–93
  exercise in, 198–99
  muscle awareness technique in, 190–
  92
  nutrition in, 195–98
  pleasure breaks in, 189–90
  priortizing in, 188–89
  relaxation response in, 190, 194–95
  restructuring in, 187
  self-talk in, 187–88
  visual imaging in, 193–94
*Stress Management for the Healthy Type
  A* (Roskies), 173
Success ethic, 74–75, 78–80
Success need
  child, 65–66
  parent, 32, 37

Sugar, stress reaction to, 197
Superachiever parent, 29–30, 31–40
Superlatives, global, 151–52
Support group
  for child, 54
  for parent, 52–53
Surarez, Edward, 99–100

Teacher relationship
  competition fostering, 58–59
  disruptive behavior and, 62
  expectations, high and, 20, 56, 57, 58, 61
  misperception of brash behavior, 59–60
  pressuring, 57–58
  star status and, 61
Temperament, reactive, 5–6, 23, 184
Test anxiety, 36
Testosterone levels, 93
Thorenson, Carl, 8, 17, 79
Time urgency, 188–89
*Treating Type A Behavior and Your Heart* (Friedman and Ulmer), 173
*Trusting Heart, The, The Great News About Type A* (Williams), 98
Truthfulness, problem with, 40–41, 42
Type A, introduction of term, 96–97
Type A behavior, negative
  and heart disease. *See* Heart disease risk
  insecurity in, 16, 17, 116. *See also* Self-esteem
  moral myopia in, 45–46, 155–56
  parental defenses against, 107–17
  parenting styles and, 35–37, 41–42, 44–46, 52
  personality traits and, 23–28
  significant others and. *See* Caregiver relationship; Peer relationship; Teacher relationship
  sky-high goals and, 6–7, 17–18, 21–28
  social trends and. *See* Society
  temperament and, 5–6, 23, 184
Type A behavior, positive
  esteem building elements in, 7–8, 101–02
  perspective building elements in, 8–9
  *See also* Child-centered communication; Discipline, respect-oriented; Goals, realistic; Stress management
*Type A Behavior Pattern & Your Heart* (Friedman and Rosenman), 94, 97
Type A characteristics, 3, 4–5, 15

accumulation, 168, 170
achievement striving, 22, 23, 26, 35, 44, 52, 59, 64, 71, 87, 97, 168, 170, 173
acting out, 36, 128, 142
aggression, 100, 158, 168, 170
attention-getting, 165–66, 170
blood pressure levels, 10, 27, 45, 92, 100
brashness, 59–60
cholesterol levels, 27, 45, 92, 100
competence, 3, 17, 19–20, 49–50
competitiveness, 6, 25–26, 42–46, 59–60, 71, 94, 97, 158
compulsiveness, 189
depression, 28, 50, 52
disruption, 62
distrust, 24, 112
dominance (leadership), 3, 158, 159, 168, 170, 174
endurance, 170, 174–75
impatience, 6, 26–27, 36, 94, 116–17
intelligence, 3, 17
modesty, excessive, 72
moral myopia, 45–46, 155–56
overcommitment, 26–27, 36, 39–40, 115
psychological reactivity, 5–6, 23, 184
psychosomatic complaints, 50, 52
success need, 65–66
time urgency, 188–89
*See also* Anger and hostility; Anxiety; Self-Exteem; Stress
Type A effect. *See* Expectations, high

Ulcers, 98
Ulmer, Diane, 173

Values
  assessment training (VAT), 169–72
  clarification, 175–81
  competitive, 42–46
  societal, 7, 8–9, 19, 87–90
  Type A, 168–69
  vehicles for changing, 181–82
*Values Clarification: Practical Strategies for Teachers* (Simon), 175
Ventilation strategy, 116
Visual imaging, 193–94
Vitamin A, 196
Vitamin B-complex, 197
Vitamin D, 197
Vitamin E, 197
Vitamin K, 197
Vitamins, food sources of, 196–97

Water consumption, nutrition and, 198
Weidner, Gerdi, 42
Western Collaborative Study, 96, 97
Whelan, Carol, 20, 70

Williams, Redford, 24, 98
Winning, 168
Wolfe, Tom, 77